you know you're in
florida when...

Some Other Books in the Series

You Know You're in Arizona When . . .

You Know You're in Illinois When . . .

You Know You're in Kansas When . . .

You Know You're in Michigan When . . .

You Know You're in Minnesota When . . .

You Know You're in New Hampshire When . . .

You Know You're In Series

you know you're in
florida when...

101 Quintessential Places, People, Events, Customs, Lingo, and Eats of the Sunshine State

David Grimes

INSIDERS' GUIDE®

GUILFORD, CONNECTICUT
AN IMPRINT OF THE GLOBE PEQUOT PRESS

INSIDERS' GUIDE®

Copyright © 2006 Morris Book Publishing, LLC.

Text design and illustrations by Linda R. Loiewski.

Library of Congress Cataloging-in-Publication Data
Grimes, David, 1952-
    You know you're in Florida when—101 quintessential places, people, events, customs, lingo, and eats of the Sunshine State / David Grimes. — 1st ed.
            p. cm. — (You know you're in series)
    Includes index.
    ISBN 0-7627-3902-9
    1. Florida—Miscellanea. 2. Florida—Description and travel—Miscellanea. I. Title.
II. Series.
    F311.6.G75 2005
    975.9—dc22
                                            2005014170

Manufactured in the United States of America
First Edition/First Printing

To Teri

about the author

David Grimes has lived in Florida for 30 years without any serious mishaps, which is pretty remarkable if you think about it. He is a columnist for the *Sarasota Herald-Tribune* and has written or cowritten several books, including *Tourists, Retirees and Other Reasons to Stay in Bed* and *Florida Curiosities.* David lives in Bradenton with his wife, Teri, and two incontinent pugs.

to the reader

You will notice, while reading this book, that there is an entry about love bugs, those amorous black flies that end their lives by splatting against your windshield (it's sort of like *Romeo and Juliet,* only much messier), but there is no entry about Lynyrd Skynyrd, the legendary Jacksonville-based band that gave the world the immortal rock anthem "Freebird."

I cannot really explain this other than to say that, having lived in Florida for 30 years, I have developed a deep, personal relationship with love bugs, but in all that time Johnny Van Zant has never once attempted to clog my radiator.

What I'm trying to say, I guess, is that the 101 entries in this book are totally subjective and ripe for second-guessing, even by me. What I've tried to do is give you a taste of this crazy, maddening, terrifying, beautiful, and never-for-a-minute-dull place called Florida. If you're a recent transplant to the Sunshine State, consider this a primer for your new home.

As you will discover, there is much more to Florida than Disney World. (The Rodent Empire, in fact, makes up less than 1 percent of the book.) Florida is oranges and lobsters and Key lime pie. It's cockroaches and mosquitoes and fire ants. It's Marjorie Stoneman Douglas and *Miami Vice* and Jackie Gleason.

I hope this book inspires you to go out and discover your own 101 favorite things about Florida.

And if you run into Johnny Van Zant, please apologize for me and tell him he will definitely be included in the second edition, assuming there is one.

you know you're in
florida when...
...you're sweating like a pig

The fact that most people are able to live through a Florida summer without melting into a puddle of goo is due, in a large part, to John Gorrie, the inventor of air-conditioning.

Some people might quibble that Gorrie did not invent air-conditioning, but rather the first ice machine. Well, the principles are the same, so the quibblers can just go annoy someone else.

In 1842 Gorrie, an Apalachicola medical doctor, invented an ice machine as a result of experiments to lower patients' fevers by cooling their hospital rooms. The scientific principle—heating a gas by compressing it, cooling it by sending it through radiating coils, and then expanding the gas to cool it further—is the same principle used in refrigerators and air conditioners today.

The story is that Gorrie was trying to make a machine to cool hospital rooms, but the thing kept freezing up and spewing out ice. Although Gorrie was granted the first U.S. patent for mechanical refrigeration in 1851, he never profited from it. Willis Haviland Carrier, of Carrier air-conditioning fame, wound up making all the money.

Air-conditioning:

An Apalachicola man's invention that makes Florida summers bearable.

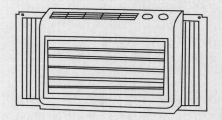

But Gorrie's contribution to Southern comfort was so monumental that the grateful citizens of Apalachicola built a museum in his honor (46 Sixth Street; 850–653–9347). It's a modest one-room building that tells the story of Gorrie's life and also contains a model of his air conditioner, ice maker, or refrigerator—whatever you want to call it.

If you've been out pulling weeds on an August day and you step into an air-conditioned building, it's unlikely that you'll be all that concerned with semantics.

you know you're in
florida when...
...you see gators everywhere

Florida is nicknamed the Sunshine State, but it could just as easily be called the Gator State.

After years of federal protection, gator populations have rebounded spectacularly until, today, there are an estimated one million of the scaly critters swimming in our lakes, rivers, ponds, and (occasionally) our backyard swimming pools.

While gators may symbolize Florida (the name is synonymous with the University of Florida) and tourists may love to gawk at them, residents and gators sometimes have a rocky relationship. The Florida Fish and Wildlife Conservation Commission receives an average of 15,000 complaints a year from people who feel threatened by one or more of the reptiles.

As Florida's population explodes, human/ alligator interactions have become more frequent. Every pond in every subdivision that's big enough to float an alligator probably has one. That means it's not uncommon to find a gator basking in your backyard or sunning himself on your pool deck. They've also been known to lumber into your garage. And, believe it or not, there have been reports of a gator turning up in a homeowner's shower stall and another one crawling into a bedroom while the homeowners slept. (The husband called 911 on his cell phone while perched atop his dresser.)

While this may sound exotic to tourists, it's less so when you consider that gators can grow to 14 feet in length and weigh 1,000 pounds. Countless pet dogs have fallen prey to "nuisance" gators, and while human fatalities are rare, 13 people have been killed by alligators since 1948.

But Floridians are biting back. There are now more than 30 alligator farms in the state. All in all, they produce around 300,000 pounds of meat and 15,000 skins.

We don't know how many wallets that translates to, but it's a lot.

Alligators:

The University of Florida football team is named after them, and at one million strong, these reptiles almost outnumber tourists.

Why are Apalachicola oysters famous? Those who love to eat them (raw, preferably) say it's their size, plumpness, and salty hint-of-the-sea flavor that makes them special.

Marine biologists say the oysters' size and abundance can be attributed to the perfect mixing in Apalachicola Bay of fresh water from the Apalachicola River with salty water from the Gulf of Mexico.

Whatever the reason, in Apalachicola, the oyster is king. The tiny town (population 2,200) in the Panhandle provides 90 percent of the oysters consumed in Florida and 1 of every 10 eaten in the whole country.

It's a tough business. Heavy iron tongs are needed to pry the oysters from their beds in the bay. Boats break down. Fuel prices climb. A heavy rain can mess things up, much less a hurricane. Then there's pollution, which has caused the state to temporarily close down oystering operations several times over the past 20 years. Because of the fear of bacterial contamination, many people today refuse to eat raw oysters.

Apalachicola Oysters:

A tiny town in the Panhandle is a huge producer of these salty delights from the sea.

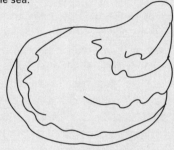

That concern is understandable, but also rather sad. Because once you've eaten a fat, cold Apalachicola oyster on the half shell you'll . . . well, you'll want another.

While some purists prefer no adornment whatsoever, we like ours with a drop or two of pepper sauce and a squeeze of lemon. For a side dish, we recommend Saltines.

Beer's not a bad idea, either. In a frosted mug, if you please.

No matter where you are in Florida, you are never more than 60 miles away from a beach. Which is understandable, considering that 1,200 miles of Florida's 1,800-mile coastline is sandy beach.

Four of the top 10 beaches in the United States in 2004 were located in Florida, according to Dr. Stephen Leatherman, director of the International Hurricane Center at Florida International University. (He swears he's unbiased.) They are: Fort DeSoto Park (#2), Caladesi Island State Park (#4), Crescent Beach at Siesta Key (#7), and Cape Florida State Recreation Area (#9).

Dr. Leatherman's rankings are based on 50 criteria, ranging from water temperature to sand softness to the amount of toilet paper floating in the water. (One has to assume that one sheet of misguided Charmin automatically disqualifies you from the Top 10.)

With all due respect to Dr. Leatherman and his 50 criteria, Florida's beaches can be broken down into three basic types. The beaches on the Gulf coast tend to consist of softer, whiter sand. The water is generally clear and the waves are usually small. (Except when a hurricane comes ashore.)

Panhandle beaches, with their many sand dunes, are some of the prettiest and most secluded, especially in the summer.

Beaches on the Atlantic coast tend to consist of coarser, darker sand. Waves are sometimes big enough to surf, but the water can be murky. However, you've got more young people and better nightlife, so it's all a matter of personal choice.

Beach sand along the northeast coast of Florida, especially on Daytona Beach, is hard-packed to the point that you can drive on it in some places.

Which is great if you're into that sort of stuff.

Beaches:

Florida is basically one big, long spit of sand, so it stands to reason we have the best beaches. We rate them for your convenience.

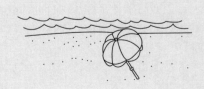

Pensacola has been dubbed the "Cradle of Naval Aviation" for good reason.

The world's first naval air station was built in this Panhandle town in 1914, and today Pensacola is the home of the Blue Angels precision flying team and the equally impressive National Museum of Naval Aviation.

After World War II, Admiral Chester Nimitz ordered the formation of a precision flying team to maintain the public's interest in naval aviation. The team was almost named the Blue Lancers until a pilot saw a magazine advertisement for a New York nightclub called the Blue Angel. Flying a variety of ever-faster Navy fighter jets, the Blue Angels have awed and entertained more than 300 million spectators at air shows dating back to 1946.

From March through November you can watch the Blue Angels practice at Pensacola Naval Air Station's Sherman Field. The free exhibitions are held Tuesday and Wednesday mornings (weather permitting). They give you a chance to get an up-close look as the pilots of the mighty blue-and-gold F/A-18 Hornets perform their death-defying acrobatics just a few feet above the tarmac. (For more information about the shows, call 850–452–2583 or visit www.navy.com/blueangels.)

Blue Angels:

Pensacola is the home of this world-famous precision flying team. Best of all, you can watch them practice for free.

After watching the Blue Angels, it's a short stroll to the National Museum of Naval Aviation. More than 150 old and new aircraft are on display here and there's also a full-size replica of a World War II aircraft carrier flight deck. If your stomach is strong, crawl into the IMAX flight simulator to find out what it feels like to take off in a Hornet, fly at more than 150 mph, and land on the deck of a carrier.

For the less adventuresome, we recommend a visit to nearby Santa Rosa Island. The beaches are soft and white, and the sunsets are very easy on the stomach.

you know you're in
florida when...
... you're in the lap of luxury

In 1904 a room at The Breakers started at $4.00 a night. Expensive, yes, but keep in mind that the sum included three meals a day.

Today the cheapest room in the palatial Palm Beach hotel goes for $400 a night. (If you have to ask what the most expensive room goes for, you can't afford it.)

Like so much of the east coast of Florida, The Breakers can attribute its existence to the redoubtable Henry Flagler. A Standard Oil magnate, Flagler built a system of rail-roads on the east coast, opening up that part of Florida to tourism and development.

Presumably so he'd have a nice place to stay while counting his money, Flagler built the first hotel on the southeast coast of Florida, the Royal Poinciana, in 1894. Located in Lake Worth, the hotel quickly began drawing the rich and famous to what would become Palm Beach.

In 1896 Flagler built a second hotel, the Palm Beach Inn, next to the Royal Poinciana but closer to the ocean. Guests were soon requesting rooms "by the breakers." When the Palm Beach Inn was expanded, Flagler renamed it The Breakers.

Fire destroyed the hotel twice. The hotel that stands today opened in 1927 and is as much an art gallery as a place for people to eat and sleep. Modeled after the Villa

Medici in Rome, The Breakers has hand-painted ceilings in its 200-foot-long lobby and its public rooms. The painting and ornamentation was done by 75 artists shipped in from Italy.

The Breakers Hotel:

In the old days The Breakers was a refuge for the rich and famous. Today The Breakers is a refuge for the rich and famous. Who says nothing stays the same?

The hotel is enormous, with 560 rooms and a staff of 1,800. There is an 18-hole golf course on the hotel grounds and also a 20,000-square-foot spa overlooking the ocean.

Dinner in the elegant L' Escalier restaurant is, unfortunately, not included in the price of your room.

you know you're in
florida when...
...you're dancing to the Coral Reefers

Perhaps nobody symbolizes the laid-back spirit of Key West more than singer/songwriter Jimmy Buffett.

In fact, most people are of the opinion that the "Margaritaville" he sings about in his most popular song is Key West. Buffett himself plays it coy; he says Margaritaville is "less a place than a state of mind." Maybe. But Buffett, who's been a Key West resident since the early 1970s, wrote "Margaritaville" in five minutes while sipping a margarita in the Key West bar, Old Anchor Inn. He said he was inspired by the throngs of tourists on the street outside the bar and the crowded highway. (If true, this has to be the first and only time that anyone has drawn artistic inspiration from gridlock.)

Buffett, born in Pascagoula, Mississippi, in 1946, was not always a troubadour for the Hawaiian-shirt and flip-flop crowd. His dream was to be a country singer. He moved to Nashville in the late 1960s, but the two albums he recorded there failed to sell. After another failed gig in Miami, Buffett took the advice of his friend Jerry Jeff Walker and moved to Key West.

The rest, as they say, is just a Cheeseburger in Paradise.

Though Buffett has several platinum albums to his credit, it's his live concerts that have really cemented his reputation. At 58 years

Jimmy Buffett:

Troubadour of the laid-back lifestyle, this popular singer/songwriter has left big footprints in the Florida sand.

of age, he remains one of the most popular performers in the country. His legions of fans, called Parrot Heads for their colorful tropical headgear, seldom miss a show.

Buffett has other interests besides music. He owns a chain of Margaritaville Cafes (the original is on Duval Street), and he's also a sailor, a pilot, a best-selling novelist *(Where is Joe Merchant?)*, and a children's-book author *(The Jolly Mon)*.

If you want to follow Buffett's search for his lost shaker of salt, try the 90-minute Trails of Margaritaville tour through Old Key West (call 305–292–2040). You get to visit several of Buffett's old haunts, beginning with Captain Tony's Saloon.

Cape Canaveral has been such a big deal over the past 55 years that the entire chunk of the east Florida coast from Melbourne to Titusville is now known as the Space Coast.

Cape Canaveral's history began long before the United States started shooting monkeys into space. Ponce de Leon "discovered" the place in 1513. The word *canaveral* means "canebrake" in Spanish, supposedly because one of the Indians living in the area (who apparently did not wish to be discovered) shot a conquistador with an arrow made of cane.

People began launching bigger things at the Cape in July 1950, when *Bumper 8,* a modified German V-2 rocket, took to the sky. Alan Shepard, the first American in space, blasted off on May 5, 1961, but the Cape really hit the big time a couple of weeks later when President John F. Kennedy threw down the Cold War gauntlet and announced that the U.S. would put a man on the moon—and bring him back, too!—before the end of the decade.

Working furiously to meet the deadline, NASA launched *Apollo 11* on July 16, 1969. America had officially won the Space Race, and we could finally lean back and say, "Take that, *Sputnik!*"

On November 28, 1963, six days after President Kennedy's assassination, new President Lyndon Johnson announced that the

Cape Canaveral:

Located in the heart of the Space Coast, this is where America shoots for the moon and the stars.

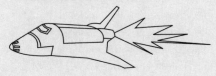

Cape would henceforth be called Cape Kennedy in honor of the president's commitment to the space program. This didn't sit well with the folks who lived in the town of Cape Canaveral, and the place eventually reverted to its original name in 1973.

To learn more about our space program's victories and disasters, spend some time at the Kennedy Space Center Visitor Complex (Highway 405, Orsino; 321–449–4444; www.kennedyspacecenter.com). Here you can strap in and experience an interactive space flight simulator at the Astronaut Hall of Fame, touch a piece of Mars, board the Space Shuttle Explorer, watch an IMAX movie about space walks (this one made us a little queasy), and even meet a real astronaut. Best of all, you can watch an actual rocket launch.

you know you're in
florida when...
...you're surrounded by psychics

There is no truth to the rumor that there is a closet full of ectoplasm inside Cassadaga's Colby Memorial Temple.

And even if there were, the stuff would not be the greenish slime of *Ghostbusters* fame, but rather "gray and smoky, with the feel of cobwebs," according to the Rev. Jim Watson, an ordained Cassadaga Spiritualist minister who claims to have seen the stuff.

Located between Orlando and Daytona Beach, the tiny village of Cassadaga bills itself as the Psychic Center of the World and, more defensibly, the Oldest Spiritualist Center in the South. Now the home of around 100 more-or-less permanent residents, Cassadaga was founded in 1894 by George P. Colby, a New York Spiritualist who was told by a medium that he would one day establish a Spiritualist community in the South. According to legend, Colby followed his Indian spirit guide, Seneca, through the Florida wilderness until he came to the precise spot he had seen in his séance, which today is on the outskirts of Deltona, within whiffing distance of the exhaust fumes of Interstate 4.

The Cassadaga Spiritualist Camp, situated on 57 acres of rolling woodland, is a tightly knit community of Spiritualists, mediums, psychics, and healers. (If you're looking for fortune tellers, tarot card readers, and crystal ball gazers, their shops are on the other side of the street.)

Spiritualists believe in continuous life and connection with the spiritual world. Needless to say, the camp is a popular place to visit at Halloween, and lots of ghost stories are based in Cassadaga.

But during daylight hours Cassadaga is a quaint, non-ghostly assemblage of lovely late-19th- and early-20th-century homes. It was added to the National Register of Historic Places in 1991. The Cassadaga Hotel—built in 1901, destroyed by fire in 1925, and rebuilt in 1927—is a charming building with rockers spaced about its wrap-around porch. After a haircut and lunch at the hotel, you can wander across the street to the Spiritualist Camp for a psychic reading (about $40) or a regression into a past life (about $200). Just watch out for the ectoplasm.

Cassadaga:

The so-called Psychic Center of the World is so small you could drive by it without noticing. What, exactly, does ectoplasm look like?

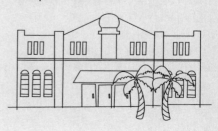

you know you're in
florida when...
... you feel you've gone back in time

It can be hard to find the "real" Florida in Florida anymore, what with our burgeoning population and new developments going up faster than you can say "gated community."

Cedar Key, though not entirely immune to condo lust, retains the Old Florida look and feel about as well as any place in the state. Isolated in the sparsely populated Big Bend region about 50 miles west of Gainesville, Cedar Key was first settled in the early 1840s and quickly blossomed into one of Florida's busiest port cities. The big industry was pencil-making, using the abundant cedar trees that gave the key its name. When the cedar trees were all gone, the resilient residents made ends meet by doing a little fishing and catering to the needs of a few tourists.

Not a great deal has changed to this day. The town has no beaches to speak of and no roller coasters (think of Cedar Key as the anti-Disney), so the tourists who visit this out-of-the-way hamlet (population 900) come to browse the shops and galleries, dine at the town's many top-notch seafood restaurants on Dock Street (farm-raised clams are a specialty), or just savor the unspoiled beauty of the place. (Cedar Key, which is actually located on Way Key, is the only occupied key in a chain of 12 islands of varying size.)

Bird-watchers will want to visit the Cedar Keys National Wildlife Refuge (www.fws .gov/cedarkeys), which you can reach by kayak or ferry.

If you like festivals, try visiting Cedar Key during the Sidewalk Art Festival in April or the Seafood Festival in October. If you're into solitude, take a trip to Cedar Key on a blustery winter day. It will just be you, the wind, and maybe a few flitting ghosts from Florida's frontier past.

Cedar Key:

Abe Lincoln's pencils might have been made here. The cedar trees are long gone, but a sense of history is still in the air.

you know you're in
florida when...
...you become a defender of chickens' rights

Katha Sheehan describes herself as a "defense attorney" for Key West's flocks of free-roaming chickens.

"Wild chickens have lived here for at least 200 years," said Sheehan, known locally as the Chicken Lady. "Pirates probably brought the first ones to use as fighting cocks; they're part of our history. People complain about the crowing and the way they scratch around in their gardens, but chickens do a lot of good, too."

Sheehan says the wild chickens, which number in the thousands, eat poisonous scorpions and centipedes, ticks, cockroaches, and termites. They are also a colorful—if somewhat noisy—symbol of Key West's laid-back, anything-goes lifestyle, she says.

The trouble is that the chickens act like they own the place, and that brings them into conflict with cars, bicycles, and homeowners who do not wish to be awakened by raucous crowing at 4:00 A.M. Sometimes the fowl are the victims of foul play, and when that happens the Chicken Lady takes the injured bird back to her combination souvenir shop, animal hospital, and petting-zoo called The Chicken Store (1229 Duval Street; 305–294–0070; www.thechicken store.com).

At any time, between 3 and 70 chickens might be rehabbing at The Chicken Store.

The Chicken Lady:

This Key West woman defends the rights of free-ranging chickens. Be advised that poultry jokes are a no-no.

Sheehan, an animal lover and former (unsuccessful) candidate for mayor, wouldn't have it any other way. "Someone needs to stand up for the chickens," she says.

When we spoke to Sheehan, she was tending to a chicken and a rabbit that had grown up together. The rabbit went by the name of Adrian, and the chicken, much to Sheehan's chagrin, was named Barbie Q. Chicken.

"I don't care for that," she sniffed. "We prefer non-culinary chicken humor around here."

you know you're in
florida when...
...you get a letter from St. Nick

Florida might not be the first state that comes to mind when you think of Christmas. (The palm trees, warm weather, and decided lack of snow might have something to do with this.)

But that doesn't mean the Sunshine State lacks the Christmas spirit. There is a small town in Orange County that is actually called Christmas. In the 1930s the post office near Fort Christmas began adding Christmas tree postmarks to letters. Today, during the holiday season, about 250,000 pieces of mail are sent through the post office from people desiring that postmark.

Since the 1970s the Kennedy Space Center has made a shuttle landing strip available on Christmas Eve for Santa Claus "in the event of a reindeer problem or mechanical difficulty." (So far, Santa has completed his rounds without having to make an emergency landing.)

Florida also is a player in the Christmas tree business. More than 120,000 trees are shipped from the state each year.

And did you know that the first Christmas Mass in America was celebrated in 1539 near what is now Tallahassee, by Spanish conquistador Hernando de Soto?

Christmas:

The post office in this small central Florida town has the holiday spirit 365 days a year.

Just because snow doesn't fall from the sky often in Florida doesn't mean we can't make some. The city of Kissimmee holds an annual Holiday Extravaganza on its lakefront that features rides, games, a lighted parade, and, yes, 20 tons of honest-to-goodness snow. Or at least its manufactured equivalent. For more information on the Holiday Extravaganza, call (407) 933–8368.

you know you're in
florida when...
...you're smokin'

On any given Saturday night, Ybor City is aswarm with young people partying inside and outside the many bars and nightclubs lining Seventh Avenue.

It's unlikely that many know—or care—about Ybor City's history and the reason for its existence. From 1886 until roughly the time of the Depression, Ybor (pronounced "EE-bore") City was known as the Cigar Capital of the World. At its height, Ybor City had more than 140 cigar factories employing 12,000 *tablatures* (cigar makers) and producing more than 250 million fine, hand-rolled cigars a year.

Ybor City was carved out of several thousand acres of swampland and palmetto scrub east of Tampa by renowned Cuban cigar makers Don Ignacio Haya and Don Vicente Martinez Ybor. In 1886 the two men, both Cuban exiles, decided to move their operation to the Tampa area because of labor problems in Key West. With the assistance of Tampa city officials, Haya and Ybor soon built the largest cigar factory in the world. Other cigar makers in Havana, Key West, and the northeastern United States moved their operations to Tampa to take advantage of cheap labor and the warm, humid climate that served as a natural humidor for the delicate tobacco leaves.

Cuban, Italian, German, and Spanish immigrants poured in until Ybor City at one point had five times the population of Tampa. Hand-rolling cigars is slow, painstaking work, which could explain the tradition of the *lector*, or reader, in the factories. A man, paid by his fellow workers, would sit on a platform and read aloud while everyone else rolled cigars. In the mornings he'd report current events from newspaper and magazines. In the afternoons he'd act out the great novels of Cervantes, Zola, and Hugo.

The great Ybor City cigar industry faded after about 50 years due to mechanization, the burgeoning popularity of cigarettes, and the Depression.

Today wrought-iron street lamps and brick streets remind tourists of the glory days of Ybor City. Assuming they can see them through all the 'clubbers.

Cigars:

Ybor City was once the place to go for hand-rolled cigars; now it's all about entertainment.

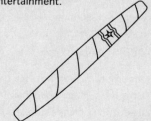

you know you're in
florida when...
...you're under the big top

Sarasota's circus heritage began in 1927, when John Ringling moved the winter headquarters of the Ringling Brothers and Barnum and Bailey Circus from Bridgeport, Connecticut, to this sleepy little town on the Gulf coast.

To say the decision rocked Sarasota's world would be an understatement. Circus stars such as Lou Jacobs, Emmett Kelly, and the Flying Wallendas became full-time residents. Jugglers and acrobats practiced on the white sands of nearby Lido Key, and Ringling even loaned some of his circus elephants to help build the bridge linking the mainland to St. Armands Key. (Appropriately enough, the road connecting the two is called John Ringling Causeway.)

The circus quickly became the biggest tourist attraction in the state. In 1951 Cecil B. DeMille brought a huge production company to town to film the Academy Award–winning movie *The Greatest Show on Earth,* starring Charlton Heston, Gloria Graham, and Cornel Wilde. Many Ringling performers and local residents had parts in the blockbuster. The world premiere of the movie was in Sarasota and was heralded with a parade down Main Street, complete with elephants and giraffes.

The circus so permeated local life that in 1950, Sarasota High School expanded its physical education program to include high-wire and trapeze instruction, acrobatics, and even a course on how to be a clown. The resulting Sailor Circus, still in existence today, was featured in the Warner Brothers film *Under the Big Top.*

The circus moved south to Venice in 1960 and disappeared from the state entirely in 1999. Venice's Clown College, the place you went to learn how to throw a pie and walk in size-30 shoes, closed its doors after 25 years in 1993.

About all that's left of Sarasota's circus heritage now is the Ringling Museum of the Circus, located next to the John and Mable Ringling Museum of Art, and Cà d'Zan, the opulent 32-room, recently restored Ringling mansion. For information on all three attractions, call (941) 359–5700 or visit www.ringling.org.

Circus:

John Ringling brought the circus to Sarasota in 1927. The Big Top is gone, but high school students keep the past alive.

Florida sided with the Confederacy during the Civil War but played a relatively minor role in the action. Some historians have called Florida "the forgotten state of the Confederacy."

No decisive battles were fought on Florida soil, mainly because the state's small population and lack of industry made it strategically unimportant to either side. Florida's main contributions to the Confederate war effort were salt, produced by boiling and evaporating sea water, and beef to help feed the troops.

The biggest Civil War battle in Florida occurred on February 20, 1864, near the town of Olustee, about 15 miles east of Lake City. A Union force of 5,500 soldiers and 16 cannon were met by a well-positioned Confederate force of approximately the same number. The battle raged for four to six hours in a sparse pine forest that offered little cover. When the smoke cleared, the Union had suffered 1,861 casualties to the Confederates' 946. This resounding Rebel victory—by far the biggest in Florida—has the dubious distinction of being one of the bloodiest battles of the Civil War in proportion to the number of troops involved.

The Olustee Battlefield Historic State Park—Florida's first state park—is open

Civil War:

Most of the action passed the state by, but Florida Confederates showed up big in key battles.

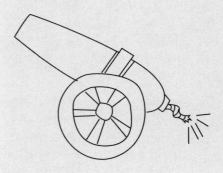

free to the public (call 386–758–0400). Battle reenactments, held every February, pay tribute to the three African-American units that fought at Olustee on the side of the Union.

To the west, just south of Tallahassee, is the Natural Bridge Battlefield Historic State Park (call 850–922–6007). That battle, fought March 4–6, 1865, was also won by the Rebs and preserved Tallahassee as the only Confederate capital east of the Mississippi never to fall into Union hands.

you know you're in
florida when...
...you see something dart under the sink

First off, despite what you may have heard, I did not scream like a little baby.

However, I think it's understandable that when you're confronted with a cockroach the size of a penny loafer, you register some emotion. I mean, what would you do if you're watching TV and some . . . some *thing* meanders across the screen? (I'm not talking about one of those annoying news crawls.)

So, yes, I did express surprise, but I most definitely did not whack my head on the ceiling, as some people have suggested. True, the mashed potatoes and meat loaf on my plate did go flying, but I think most people would react with similar alarm if a cockroach the size of a toaster oven suddenly interrupted their enjoyment of a *Roseanne* rerun.

You know what I think is funny? I think it's funny that people in Florida refer to cockroaches as "palmetto bugs," as if a euphemism is going to make anyone feel better about insects the size of manhole covers skittering across their kitchen floor.

Cockroaches love warm, humid places, which is why Florida is paradise to the suckers. Sure, keeping your house clean helps, but cockroaches will get into your trash, clamber up your plumbing, and even go after the glue in the binding of your books if they can't find anything better to eat. You can elect to battle the bugs yourself, if you wish, and you may even win. But most people find it's easier to hire a pest-control company and get monthly sprayings.

Either way, Floridians either come to accept cockroaches as part of the ecosystem, or they move back to Minnesota and deal with the snow.

Personally, I think I can learn to live in peace with cockroaches as long as they do not grow to the size of a Ford Taurus and fly around my living room while I'm trying to watch *The Simpsons*. Because that just makes me angry.

Cockroaches:

Florida cockroaches use New York roaches for toothpicks. We call ours "palmetto bugs" because we're unable to cope with reality.

16

you know you're in
florida when...
...you hear waves crashing in your head

A Key West resident refers to himself as a "conch." The proper way to pronounce this is "conk," as in, "If you don't pass me that sunscreen, I'll conk you on the head."

While that much knowledge will be enough to get you by on most Key West beaches, there actually is a story behind the name. A conch is a type of whelk, or large marine snail. If you hold a conch's shell to your ear, you can hear the ocean. (It works better if the marine snail is not still occupying its shell.)

In the old days, conch meat was a staple of a Key Wester's diet. (Big Macs had not been invented yet.) The chewy meat was eaten raw, marinated in vinegar, or fried. This could explain why lifelong Key Westers are so tough.

Conchs (the sea-critter variety) were eventually over-harvested to the point that all Florida conch meat now comes from the Bahamas. That is fitting because some of the first conchs (the human variety) were British sympathizers during Revolutionary War days who hid in the Bahamas after announcing that they'd rather go to war than eat conch. (Many tourists, upon eating the rubbery conch meat for the first time, have made the same vow.) When Florida became a territory of the United States in 1821, Bahamians involved in the salvage

Conchs:

Chewy whelk meat gives Key Westers their name and is also great in chowder.

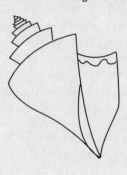

industry moved to the Keys and brought the conch label with them.

Whatever the origin of the word, it is considered a good thing to be a conch, at least in Key West. In times past, families would put a conch shell on a stick to announce the birth of a baby. Today city officials declare someone an "official conch" if he or she does something praiseworthy of a civic nature, and new residents are referred to as "freshwater conchs."

Either way, it's better than being called a *Strombus gigas,* the Latin name for the Queen conch. Though we're guessing they taste pretty much the same.

you know you're in
florida when...
...you're surrounded by gigantic coral blocks

Edward Leedskalnin was so in love with Agnes Scuffs that he built her a house made out of coral.

At the Coral Castle in Homestead, the walls are made out of coral and the gates are made out of coral. There are coral rocking chairs, a coral bed, a coral table in the shape of a heart, coral fountains, and even a kind of coral stockade in case any children they might have (and maybe even Agnes) were ever in need of discipline.

One can only imagine what Ed would have built if he disliked Agnes.

Actually, it's all rather romantic, in a 19th-century Latvian sort of way. In the early 1900s, when Ed was 26, he was engaged to marry Agnes, 10 years his junior. On the day before the wedding, Agnes backed out on the grounds that Ed was too old.

A broken heart affects different people in different ways. In Ed's case it inspired him to single-handedly dig out, move, and arrange 29-ton slabs of coral rock into a castle of unrequited love. The work was certainly not made any easier by the fact that Ed stood 5 feet tall, weighed 100 pounds, and was plagued by bouts of tuberculosis.

How did Ed, a wheezing squirt of a man with an elementary-school education, assemble this 11,000-ton house, the South

Coral Castle:

A little man from Latvia constructed this impressive, if highly untraditional, home for his unrequited love.

Florida equivalent of Stonehenge or the pyramids, all by himself? That is the essential and perhaps never-to-be-answered riddle of Coral Castle.

The Coral Castle story is inspiring, but also rather sad. Ed died in Miami in 1954 at age 64. Despite repeated entreaties, the love of his life, Agnes, never paid him a single visit.

For information on Coral Castle guided tours, call (305) 248–6345 or visit www.coralcastle.com.

We consider this entry a once-in-a-lifetime opportunity to use the word *zooxanthellae*.

For those of you who are not heavily into marine biology (and you know who you are), zooxanthellae are the algae that live in a symbiotic relationship with coral polyps that extract calcium and carbon dioxide from . . . oh, the heck with it. They're the stuff that gives a coral reef its pretty colors.

Florida is the only state in the continental United States that has living coral reefs. There are approximately 6,000 of the things stretching from Stuart on the Atlantic coast to the Dry Tortugas, west of Key West, in the Gulf of Mexico. The best reefs are on the Atlantic side of the Florida Keys. They have exotic/whimsical names like Carysfort Reef, Molasses Reef, and Hens and Chickens.

The problem with Florida's coral reefs is that they are too popular. Several million snorklers, scuba divers, fishermen, and boaters visit the reefs each year. Florida is the number-one dive destination in the world, 10 times more popular than number-two Australia, which has 10 times more reefs. Florida's coral reefs, which are between 5,000 and 7,000 years old and grow only 1 to 16 feet every 1,000 years, are easily damaged. Boat propellers and anchors, pollution, global warming, and people stepping on or touching the reefs cause extensive harm.

Though coral reefs may appear to be nothing more than beautifully colored and patterned rock, they are actually living things. Hundreds of thousands of coral polyps add a thin layer to the reef, then die. The outermost 1/16 of an inch of the coral reef is living polyps; the underlying layers are the calcified remains of polyps past.

Many Florida visitors get their first view of a coral reef at John Pennekamp Coral Reef State Park in Key Largo, America's first underwater park. It consists of 178 nautical square miles of reefs, sea grass beds, and mangrove swamps. Scuba, snorkeling, and glass-bottom boat trips are conducted year-round. (For more information, call 305–451–1202 or visit www.pennekamp park.com.)

Coral Reefs:

We humans are doing everything we can to ruin them, but some fabulously colorful coral reefs can still be seen in the Keys.

19

you know you're in
florida when...
...you like your sandwiches flat

The jury is still out on whether the best Cuban sandwich can be found in Tampa or Miami.

The oldest continually operated Cuban sandwich shop is the Silver Ring Cafe in Tampa, which opened in 1947. On the other hand, Tampa Cuban sandwiches contain salami, which Miami Cuban-Americans consider a sin.

Either way, there are very strict rules regarding the construction of this delectable sandwich made with ham, roast pork, cheese, and pickles. (If you ask for lettuce, tomato, onion, or, God forbid, mayonnaise on your Cuban, you may as well have the word *tourist* stenciled on your forehead. Mustard, however, is acceptable.)

The first essential ingredient is the bread. Only Cuban bread will do. Made with lard, it has the crunchy exterior and soft middle that makes Cuban sandwiches so distinctive.

The other thing you must have is a sandwich press, called a *plancha*. The sandwich is grilled in the *plancha* until the ham, pork, and pickles have cooked in their own steam. Cuban-sandwich makers get into arguments over who has the heaviest *plancha*. Like we said, a good Cuban sandwich is serious business.

The press-weight issue notwithstanding, what emerges is a toasty, flat sandwich, inside of which the ham, pork, cheese, and pickle have oozed and melted into one another until . . . sorry, we've got to stop. We're making ourselves hungry.

The first Cuban sandwich is believed to have been made by Cuban immigrants who came to the Ybor City area of Tampa in the late 1800s to work in the cigar factories.

Interestingly enough, Cubans don't eat Cuban sandwiches, or at least not Cuban sandwiches like the ones you'll find in Tampa and Miami. A *Cuban* Cuban sandwich is simply made with roast pork.

And one would like to think that real Cubans have better things to do than argue about the weight of their *planchas*.

Cuban Sandwich:

The pork is important, and so is the cheese, but the real art in making a Cuban sandwich is how flat you squash the bread.

In 1902 two cars built by famed automakers Ransom Olds and Alexander Winton raced each other on a 20-mile stretch of hard-packed sand between Ormond Beach and Daytona Beach.

The race was too close to call, but the cars had topped out at a then-mind-bending speed of 57 mph. Racing at Daytona Beach was born.

Today the Daytona 500 is one of the biggest events in sports. More than 150,000 spectators cram into the grandstands to watch the late-February race, while nearly 20 million others view the spectacle on TV.

Cars raced on the sand until 1936, when 1.5 miles of blacktop was added. The cars sped along on the pavement, then turned in the sand and raced back on the beach, creating a 3.2-mile course.

During the Depression years there was little money to waste on fancy race cars, so competitors raced in their personal cars that saw everyday use. Thus did the racing Fords and Chevys come to be known as "stock cars."

Racing in Daytona went into a slump during the war years, but it rebounded in 1959, when the track was improved and expanded into the 2.5-mile oval that remains in use today. The first 500-mile race on what

Daytona 500:

Cars don't run on the sand anymore, but this race continues to be one of the biggest sporting events of the year.

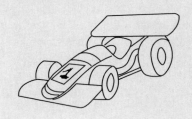

came to be known as Daytona International Speedway was won by Lee Petty, whose son, Richard, went on to win seven Daytona 500s, more than anyone else to date.

The Daytona 500 is the most prestigious event on the NASCAR circuit. (NASCAR stands for National Association of Stock Car Auto Racing.) It is the final event in a 16-day racing extravaganza known as Speedweeks.

Though some may not see the fascination of watching over-powered cars drive around in what is essentially one long, extended left turn, many others find the experience riveting.

Either way, we recommend you bring a seat cushion and a high-grade pair of ear plugs.

you know you're in
florida when...
...a mouse calls your name

Walt Disney World was almost built in St. Louis, until the head of the Busch family (of Anheuser-Busch fame) told Walt he would be crazy to build a theme park in St. Louis and not sell beer.

Then it was almost built along the Florida coast, but Walt was afraid of hurricanes and also of visitors showing up in swimsuits. (Walt Disney had very strong opinions about some things.)

Finally Walt, his brother, Roy, and General Joe Potter, whom Walt had met at the 1964 New York World's Fair, began looking at land in central Florida. "Project X" was born.

As its name implies, Project X was very secretive. Walt didn't want to tip off the locals that he was buying lots of land along the border of Orange and Osceola Counties because that would have driven up prices. Beginning in 1964, dummy corporations were set up and Disney agents began buying land under phony names. When all the deals were done, Disney owned more than 27,000 acres, or about 43 square miles, of Florida swampland. The tract is twice as large as Manhattan and about 150 times bigger than Disneyland in California. The cost: just over $5 million, making it perhaps the best land bargain since the Louisiana Purchase.

Walt died in 1966 of lung cancer, but his vision lived on. (Boy, did it ever.) Today the Walt Disney Company operates or licenses 10 theme parks on 3 continents (the newest one in Hong Kong), 35 resort hotels, 2 luxury cruise ships, a variety of TV properties (including ABC networks and ESPN), and . . . well, suffice it to say Disney owns lots of stuff.

Walt Disney World Resort, which started out as nothing more than buggy swampland, is now the top vacation destination in the world.

And in the Magic Kingdom, you still can't buy a beer.

Disney World:

The vision of one man, plus some secretive real-estate deals, resulted in the world's biggest entertainment empire.

you know you're in
florida when...
...Flipper is your friend

Dolphins (and their porpoise cousins) are abundant in the warm coastal waters of Florida, but it's still a thrill to tourists and residents alike when the sleek mammals are spotted playing in the wake of a boat or simply gliding along.

Of all the thousands of dolphins, one was singled out for everlasting fame. That dolphin is, of course, Flipper. Her real name (yes, Flipper was female) was Mitzi. For the 1963 movie bearing her stage name, Mitzi was trained at what is now the Dolphin Research Center (DRC) at mile marker 59 on Grassy Key. The movie, co-starring Chuck Connors, was also shot there.

Back in the early 1960s, the DRC was called Santini's Porpoise School. It was run by Milton Santini, a pioneer in dolphin training. Mitzi was Santini's first (and obviously most famous) pupil; she became the star of the movie and the subsequent TV series, which ran from 1964 to 1967.

Mitzi performed most of the stunts, such as towing damaged boats to shore and whacking guns out of a bad guy's hands with her nose or tail. But a "stunt double" dolphin named Mr. Gipper performed the tail-walking scenes. (Mitzi never mastered tail-walking; perhaps she deemed it unladylike.)

Dolphins:

These aquatic mammals are a common sight, but there can be only one Flipper.

Mitzi died of a heart attack in 1972 and was buried beneath a dolphin statue in the school's courtyard. The 30-foot concrete statue of a mother and baby dolphin is now maintained by the DRC, an organization devoted to research and dolphin awareness. A plaque beneath the statue reads:

> DEDICATED TO THE MEMORY OF MITZI
> THE ORIGINAL FLIPPER
> 1958–1972

Mitzi had no offspring, but Mr. Gipper did. His daughter, Tursy, is reported to be a fine tail-walker.

you know you're in
florida when...
... you think there's no such thing as too many oranges

The first thing most people do when they move to Florida is plant a citrus tree in their backyard. This is perfectly understandable and nothing to be ashamed of.

After all, what transplant from the Frozen North would not be captivated by the prospect of shuffling out to his yard on a perfect 70-degree December morning to pluck a few ripe tangelos off his very own tree?

If this is not paradise, it must be awfully close, the new homeowner imagines. And so he attempts to improve upon paradise by planting a grapefruit tree alongside his tangelo, even though he's not particularly fond of grapefruit.

And this, too, is perfectly understandable and nothing, just yet, to be ashamed of.

The new homeowner is on a roll now and perhaps envisions himself as the new citrus baron of his gated subdivision. So he plants a lime tree and a lemon tree and a Valencia orange tree and a pink grapefruit tree because even though it's still grapefruit, it's, well . . . pink.

This is no longer remotely understandable, and the homeowner should be deeply ashamed. Because in a few years, when all of his tiny new citrus trees reach maturity, the fellow who merely wanted an occasional glass of fresh-squeezed tangelo juice

Dooryard Citrus:

Those orange, grapefruit, and lime trees that seemed like such a good idea when you moved here can come back to haunt you.

with his morning bran flakes will be knee-deep in citrus.

What he failed to consider was that when the first tangelo ripens, so, too, do the other 657 tangelos on the tree. Same with the grapefruits, limes, lemons, etc.

So the homeowner gets out his calculator and figures that he must, on a daily basis, drink a minimum of 382 glasses of juice, knock back 48 margaritas, and bake 23 lemon meringue pies if he is to keep up.

And then the fruit starts to fall from the trees. *Thump. Thump.* Multiplied by a thousand. The homeowner finds himself out in his yard every day, picking up squashed, half-rotted fruit and hauling it to the curb.

It's a pain, but he tells himself that it's better than shoveling snow. And you know what? It is.

Marjory Stoneman Douglas has been called the "Mother of the Everglades." Developers and the moguls behind Big Sugar have undoubtedly called her other, less flattering things.

Born in Minnesota in 1890, Douglas moved to Miami in 1915, taking a job alongside her father at the newspaper that would eventually become the *Miami Herald.* She started out as a society reporter, but the Wellesley grad's quick mind and boundless energy soon had her tackling meatier subjects. She wrote extensively about feminism, racial justice, and conservation long before these causes became popular.

A prolific writer and riveting speaker until her death in 1998 at the age of 108, Douglas's masterpiece is her 1947 book *The Everglades: River of Grass.* Using fluid prose to describe the slow-moving sheet of water that sustains the Everglades, Douglas wrote of the terrible harm done to the 'Glades when people choked off the flow with dikes, levees, and canals.

A short, scrappy woman known to enjoy a nip of bourbon after a hard day's work, Douglas eventually got what she wanted, even if she didn't live to see it. In 2000 Congress approved the first stages of a $7.8 billion Everglades restoration project in partnership with the state of Florida.

Friends of the Everglades, an advocacy group that Douglas founded in 1970, continues to monitor the health of the 'Glades and has pressured lawmakers to follow through with the restoration plan.

The Everglades couldn't have asked for a better Mother than Douglas.

Marjorie Stoneman Douglas:

An early feminist, civil-rights advocate, and author of *The Everglades: River of Grass.* Her legacy lives on.

At the Don Garlits Museum of Drag Racing, you might actually run into Big Daddy himself.

The king of drag racing and his wife, Pat, live in a house on the grounds, and it's not unusual for Garlits to stop by the museum, chat with visitors, and maybe share a story or two about what it was like to cover a quarter-mile in 4.72 seconds at a top speed of 303.27 mph.

Garlits was given his nickname by his daughters, who used to watch him from the stands while shouting, "Go, daddy! Go, daddy! Go, daddy." A track announcer modified the chant and began calling him Big Daddy, which is a bit of a stretch since Garlits stands no taller than 5 feet, 9 inches.

The Ocala museum, which Garlits opened in 1983, contains about 150 drag racers with names like Pandemonium, Pollutionizer, and Yellow Fang. Garlits's personal cars, painted in trademark black, include Swamp Rat 22, the famous dragster that set a 1975 world speed record (250.69 mph in 5.63 seconds) that stood for seven years.

At the museum, it's rather odd to see all that power sitting in front of you, not moving. Drag racing is all about flames and smoking tires and ear-splitting noise. The cars on display are as quiet as extinct dinosaurs.

But if you're a fan of drag racing, none of that will matter. The exhibits will bring back memories of great cars and the men who drove them.

The Museum of Drag Racing is located south of Ocala at 13700 Southwest 16th Avenue. For more information, call (352) 245–8661 or visit www.garlits.com.

Drag Racing:

Don Garlits's museum in Ocala tells you everything you need to know about this turbo-charged sport.

you know you're in
florida when...
...a light bulb goes off in your head

In 1885 a light bulb went off in Thomas Edison's head: Why not build a house along the Caloosahatchee River in warm, sunny Fort Myers and say goodbye to those nasty winters in Menlo Park, New Jersey?

The result, finished a year later and dubbed "Seminole Lodge," served as a winter retreat and workplace for the prolific inventor until his death in 1931.

Designed by Edison (of course), Seminole Lodge was prefabricated in Maine before being shipped south. The house is well ventilated to deal with the hot, muggy Florida summers (Edison was apparently too busy inventing everything else to have time to tackle air-conditioning) and has several interesting features. The electric chandeliers ("electroliers") were designed by Edison and built in his own shop. The kitchen and dining room are part of the guest house because Edison suffered from stomach ulcers and didn't care for the smell of food cooking. Also, if his visitors proved tiresome, he could excuse himself after dinner and return to his own quarters, rather than having to wait for them to leave.

Edison's most famous guest was his friend and admirer Henry Ford, the automobile pioneer, who built his own winter home along the river in 1916. Both are part of the Edison-Ford Winter Estates, which offer tours every day except Thanksgiving and Christmas (call 941–334–3614 or visit www.edison-ford-estate.com).

The guided tour includes what was a working research laboratory. There's a small cot where Edison, who didn't need much sleep, took catnaps during the day. After his death in 1931, workers had to test the chemicals he had been using in the lab; the famous inventor, blessed with a prodigious memory, never bothered to label bottles.

Edison was completely deaf in his later years, and one of the most remarkable exhibits in the museum is a family phonograph. It has teeth marks on the wooden edge, where Edison would bite down on the wood and "listen" to the music through the vibrations in his jaw.

Good thing for Edison's molars that heavy metal and rap had not yet been invented.

Thomas Edison:

America's greatest inventor made his southern home in Fort Myers. The museum gives you a greater appreciation of this quirky genius.

you know you're in
florida when...
...you've got to shake that thing

Maybe the heat and humidity reminded him of his home in Tupelo, Mississippi, but for whatever reason, Elvis Presley loved performing in Florida.

The King did 17 shows in Jacksonville alone between 1955 and 1977, the year he died. One of his movies, *Follow That Dream,* was filmed in several north-central Florida locations. Interior scenes were shot in an Ocala bank building and in the Inverness courthouse.

It was at the August 10, 1956, show at Jacksonville's Florida Theater that Elvis's controversial pelvic gyrations first made national headlines. Juvenile Court Judge Marion Gooding attended the concert to see what all the fuss was about. The judge did not become an instant fan; in fact, he came away convinced that Elvis was undermining the youth of America and told Elvis that if he wiggled his hips during the second show, the judge would have him arrested.

Miffed but respectful of authority, Elvis made no movements during his second show except to wave his pinkie. The crowd, needless to say, loved it.

When doing shows in Jacksonville between 1972 and 1977, Elvis always stayed at the Hilton (now the Hilton Towers; 904–398–8800). After he left his room in the morning, hotel maids would cut up his bed sheets

Elvis:

The King was a frequent visitor to Florida. What better way to remember him than to decorate a hotel room in his honor?

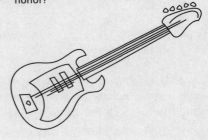

into 2-inch squares and sell them to the throngs of fans gathered outside. If you're planning on staying at the hotel and want to feel like the King for a night, ask for room 1010, otherwise known as the Elvis Room.

Another Elvis room—less expensive but considerably tackier—can be found at the Traveler's Inn in Daytona Beach (call 800–417–6466). Room 118 features leopard-pattern curtains and bedspreads, and the walls are covered with Elvis movie and concert posters. If the room is booked, you might consider staying in the Harley-Davidson room, the NASCAR room, or the Star Wars room. All can be rented for between $35 and $65, which is a small price to pay for a brush with celebrity.

As national parks go, the Everglades can be a little underwhelming.

There are no majestic mountains, no giant redwoods, and no grand canyons. About all there is to the Everglades is . . . grass.

Everglades actually means "river of grass," but it's not the kind of grass you cultivate in your backyard. It's tall, fibrous sawgrass, so named because if you walk through it without protective clothing, you will come out looking like you took second place in a knife fight.

The best way to explore the Everglades is with an airboat and an experienced guide because in this vast, trackless place, it's easy to get lost. Oddly enough, that's exactly what some of the Everglades' first inhabitants were trying to do. Seminole Indians and escaped slaves, both trying to elude capture by the U.S. Army, took refuge in the swamp in the early 1800s.

A couple of wars later, most of the Seminoles were killed or captured and sent off to dismal reservations west of the Mississippi, mainly in Oklahoma. The Seminole and Miccosukee Indians that remain in the Everglades today don't have to hide anymore; many of them are involved in the casino industry, most conspicuously the 10-story-high Miccosukee Resort and Gaming Center at the eastern edge of the swamp.

Although at 1.5 million acres it is the largest subtropical wilderness in the continental United States, the Everglades is a much different place today than it was just a century ago. In its natural state, the Everglades was a 60-foot-wide sheet of shallow water that flowed south at a snail's pace from the Kissimmee River and Lake Okeechobee over sawgrass, palmetto scrub, and oak hammocks before eventually emptying into Florida Bay. Beginning in the 1930s, canals were dug to divert the water and open up land for agriculture. Today encroaching development from the east threatens the swamp further. A vast, expensive Everglades restoration project is now in the works and may be the swamp's best hope for survival.

To learn more about the Everglades and acquaint yourself with its subtle beauties and abundant wildlife, read Marjorie Stoneman Douglas's excellent 1947 book *The Everglades: River of Grass*.

Everglades:

Dried up, planted over, and generally abused, this once-glorious swamp looks forward to better things.

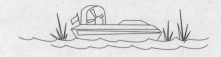

you know you're in
florida when...
... you perform the dance of the ants

You are out gardening on a fine spring morning. The sun is warm, the air is cool, and all is right with the world.

Suddenly you feel something stinging your ankle. Then another sting. Then, in an instant, your entire leg feels like it's being punctured with red-hot needles.

Allow me to introduce to you the red fire ant, otherwise known as the Scourge of the South. Like some other unpleasant things (the Macarena springs immediately to mind), fire ants came to Florida from South America, probably in the late 1920s or early 1930s. Today they rule the entire southeastern United States and recently have turned up as far north as Philadelphia.

Fire ants are not to be trifled with. They are very aggressive and each little ant stings repeatedly, injecting venom that causes burning pain and, later, tiny, itching pustules. Some people are allergic to fire ant stings. On average, six people per year die from the things.

A movie about fire ants would be too horrible to watch. Each mound contains anywhere from 10,000 to 100,000 ants. It's not uncommon to find 1,000 mounds per acre. Get enough fire ants together and they can kill a cow. Bedridden people in nursing homes have been attacked by fire ants. So have babies. Fire ants damage crops, including citrus trees. They have caused

sections of road to collapse by removing the soil underneath the asphalt. They have been known to nest in traffic lights, air conditioners, and computers, creating all sorts of havoc.

What can you do about fire ants? Not much. Commercial pesticides work (so does dousing a mound with boiling water), but reinforcement ants are close behind. Even hurricanes do not discourage fire ants. During floods, fire ants form into a ball and float along the surface of the water. If they hit the side of a canoe—or your leg—they climb aboard.

So watch where you step. When gardening, tuck your pants into your socks. And when you feel that first searing puncture, be prepared to perform the Macarena. Otherwise called the Dance of the Fire Ant.

Fire Ants:

These aggressive, stinging critters can turn gardening into an aerobic workout.

It's not clear how flamingos came to be associated with Florida, given that none of the several species of the bird are native to the Sunshine State (or anywhere else in the United States, for that matter).

It's possible that Hialeah Park racetrack, opened in 1925, had something to do with it. Now closed, Hialeah in its heyday boasted a population of more than 900 Caribbean flamingos, earning the place the title of Most Beautiful Racetrack in America.

Aside from the ubiquitous lawn ornaments, the best way to see flamingos today is at a theme park. SeaWorld and Busch Gardens have sizeable flocks, as do Jungle Gardens in Sarasota and Homossasa Springs State Park. If you're lucky, you might spy an escaped flamingo or two in Everglades National Park. Rent a canoe at—where else?—Flamingo, and bring along plenty of industrial-strength mosquito repellant.

If you're wondering how flamingos get their striking coloring, it's from the food they eat.

Certain algae and shellfish give the birds their distinctive hue, which can range from pale pink to bright red. (For flamingos in captivity, the coloring is courtesy of a special dye in their food.) Baby flamingos, possibly because they have not yet bellied up

Flamingos:

The tall pink birds that have come to symbolize Florida aren't even native to the state. We think they're cool anyway.

to the all-you-can-eat seafood bar, are a decidedly unspectacular gray or white.

Flamingo trivia: Flamingos have been around for 47 million years, or approximately how long it's been since we last won a bet at a horse track. The birds were well known in Egypt in sphinx-building times. A flamingo plays a prominent role in Aristophanes' 414 B.C. play *The Birds*.

Or so we're told; we slept through that class.

you know you're in
florida when...
...you're in the mood for something spiny

There are shellfish snobs out there who will tell you that Florida lobsters are vastly inferior to Maine lobsters, in both size and taste.

While it is true that Florida lobsters don't have claws, there are few things in life that compare to catching a few Florida lobsters and then eating them—with melted butter, of course—a few minutes later on the deck of your boat bobbing gently in the warm, clear waters of the Keys.

Florida lobsters, also called spiny lobsters because of their many sharp spines and the two sharp horns that protrude from the animals' eyes, are caught almost exclusively in the waters of Monroe County. The commercial trapping season is August 6 to March 31, during which six million pounds of lobsters are typically caught, with a value of $23 million.

Much more fun is the two-day "sport" lobster season held every year in July. Recreational divers and snorkelers by the thousands flock to the Keys, filling every available motel room and campsite. The tools of the trade are heavy gloves, a small mesh net, and a "tickle stick" used to prod the lobsters out of their rocky homes. You're apt to have better luck if you work with a partner, especially if you're new to

Florida Lobsters:

So what if they don't have any claws? These tasty crustaceans are still melted butter's best friend.

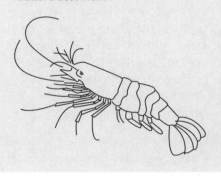

the game. Experience definitely helps in lobster hunting.

Although most Florida lobsters are caught in the Keys, the state's biggest lobster festival is in Panama City, in the Panhandle. Lobster Fest takes place every year in September and includes a fishing tournament and lots of good eatin' (for more information, call 850–235–3555).

Sorry; no Maine lobsters allowed.

you know you're in
florida when...
...you catch a glimpse of the top cat

The Florida panther is the official state mammal, and its likeness can be seen on more than a million Florida license plates.

Yet for all its popularity, very few people have actually seen a panther. A slightly smaller cousin of the mountain lion, the Florida panther is one of the most endangered species on Earth. Once abundant throughout the Southeast, fewer than 100 adult Florida panthers remain, most of them confined to Everglades National Park and Big Cypress National Preserve in southwest Florida.

Because it was (incorrectly) believed to be a major threat to livestock, the Florida panther was hunted to near-extinction in the mid-1950s. Florida schoolchildren voted the panther the state mammal in 1982, and ever since, conservation efforts have been waged on many fronts to protect the reclusive tawny cat.

Destruction of habitat is the biggest threat to the panther (males need a range of up to 400 square miles), with vehicle-related deaths coming in second. Alligator Alley, the old two-lane road that cuts through the Everglades, connecting the east and west coasts, used to be a vehicular killing ground for panthers. When Alligator Alley was converted to Interstate 75 in 1993, underpasses were constructed to aid the crossing of panthers and other wildlife.

Since then, no panthers have died on this road.

Recently Florida panthers have been mated with Western cougars in an attempt to expand and diversify the gene pool. Wildlife officials have been working quickly because the tiny panther population is starting to show the unhealthy effects of inbreeding, including heart murmurs and immune-system disorders.

A male panther weighs up to 130 pounds, female panthers around 70. They eat deer, feral hogs, raccoons, and (rarely) alligators. Visit the Florida Panther Society at www.panthersociety.org for more information.

There has never been a documented attack of a Florida panther on a human. But in rapidly developing southwest Florida, humans are squeezing panthers to death.

Florida Panther:

This rare and elusive cat can sometimes be spotted in the Everglades and other remote areas.

you know you're in
florida when...
...you're digging up a saber-toothed tiger

When people talk about fossils in Florida, they're usually speaking (unflatteringly) of the state's sizeable population of gray-haired retirees.

But Frank Garcia of Ruskin deals with different kinds of fossils. In 1983 the amateur paleontologist discovered prehistoric remains in the Leisey Shell Pit near the Little Manatee River. Eventually he would find fossils of hundreds of extinct beasts that roamed a very different Florida almost two million years ago, including saber-toothed tigers, mastodons, and giant sloths. Thirty of the fossilized animals he discovered were previously unknown to science.

Today the Leisey Shell Pit is considered the largest repository of Pleistocene-era fossils in the world. In Garcia's museum/workshop you can view the remains of ancient vultures and camels and the skull of a 50-foot-long great white shark that once swam in what we now call the Gulf of Mexico.

Garcia runs the Paleo Preserve, a nonprofit educational center on the site of the shell pit. Schoolchildren learn about Florida's prehistory and also get hands-on experience digging in the pit, where it's still fairly easy to find a bit of mastodon bone or the jagged, fossilized tooth of an ancient shark.

Garcia always enjoyed poking around for fossils in phosphate mines and abandoned shell pits. One day he discovered a skull

Fossils:

You won't find any dinosaur bones here, but Florida is still a Jurassic Park of big—and scary—extinct beasts.

that looked like it belonged to a giraffe or a camel, only it had horns like those of an antelope. It turned out that the skull belonged to a previously unknown species that scientists eventually named *Kyptoceras amatorum*. *Kyptoceras* means "horned beast," and *amatorum* means "amateur" or "lover"—after Garcia, an amateur lover of fossils.

Garcia hardly fits the stereotype of stuffy scientist. He's got a couple of bawdy Bill Clinton jokes that he'll gladly share with you, and his impersonation of Elvis is dead-on.

On a shelf, next to the massive head of an ancient crocodile, sits an unopened can of Billy Beer. Even famous fossil hunters like to have fun.

you know you're in
florida when...
...you suddenly feel young again

Today people turn back the clock with the help of Viagra and cosmetic surgery.

But in Juan Ponce de Leon's day, a simple fountain of flowing water was all that was needed to forestall the ravages of time. Unfortunately, the secret of eternal youthfulness was as ephemeral then as it is now.

Ancient Indian legends put the Fountain of Youth in a place called Bimini, north of Puerto Rico in (possibly) today's Bahama Islands. Immersing oneself in the river, spring, or fountain (or whatever it was) was supposed to make the old young and the young, well . . . damp.

Ponce de Leon, who had accompanied Columbus on the latter's second voyage in 1493, supposedly heard of the legend from the Indians. Whether he believed it is another matter. (Some cynics say that Ponce de Leon's quest was more about gold than transmutative waters; after all, the man was only 53, barely old enough for his first weave.)

In any event, Ponce de Leon commissioned three ships at his own expense and set out to find the Fountain of Gold . . . er, Youth. Unfortunately for him, the only thing he discovered was Florida. On March 27, 1513, Ponce de Leon sighted the American mainland, which, in keeping with the general perspicuity of the time, he immediately identified as an island.

Ponce de Leon may not have found the Fountain of Youth, but he did inspire a tourist attraction of the same name, which is almost as good. It is located at 11 Magnolia Avenue in St. Augustine (call 904–829–3168 or 800–356–8222). This is supposed to be the exact spot where the Spanish explorer staggered to shore on April 2, 1513, and claimed the "New World" in the name of the king. There's lots of history to be learned at the place and visitors can even sip from the Fountain's supposedly restorative waters.

Personally, we think a healthy diet and exercise are probably better bets.

Fountain of Youth:

Ponce de Leon failed to find it, but thousands of retirees in Florida are looking pretty spry.

you know you're in
florida when...
...you're getting in touch with your inner Tarzan

There are about 200 freshwater springs in Florida, but Wakulla Springs is the grand-daddy of them all.

Located about 30 miles south of Tallahassee, Wakulla Springs is the focal point of the Edward Ball Wakulla Springs State Park and Lodge. One of the largest and deepest freshwater springs in the world, Wakulla is fed by an underground river that gushes water at the rate of 400,000 gallons a minute. Divers entering the mouth of the underwater cavern often have their face masks blown off by the force of the current.

We will resist the temptation to call the waters of Wakulla Springs "gin clear," as it has been our experience that alcohol makes things less clear rather than more. Suffice it to say that the water here is really, really clear. If the light is right, you can see things on the bottom, 185 feet down. In 1850 a woman reportedly spotted the bones of a mastodon at the bottom of the springs. (No word on whether gin was involved.)

Wakulla is so deep that no one has discovered its source. In 1989 a professional cave-diving expedition into the springs was filmed for a *National Geographic* television special. Other dive teams have descended more than 300 feet into the honeycomb of limestone caves beneath the springs. At that point the cavern branches into four channels, each tunneling still deeper into the earth. That's as far as anyone's gotten.

Freshwater Springs:

Crystal-clear water and constant year-round temperatures attract everyone from snorklers to movie stars.

Wakulla Springs is also a popular hangout for slimy human-like creatures with gills, webbed feet, or other notable features. *The Creature from the Black Lagoon* was filmed here, as were *Airport '77,* the unforgettable *Joe Panther,* and several early Tarzan movies starring Johnny Weissmuller.

Like all Florida springs, the waters of Wakulla maintain a constant, year-round temperature of about 75 degrees. Jumping in is a bit of a shock, even on the hottest day. There's a 15-foot-high diving platform if you want to get it over with right away, or you can inch in a bit at a time, flapping your arms and yelling, "OhmygodIt'sCold!!"

Once you're in and swimming with the fishes, don't be surprised if you spy an occasional alligator. Hey, it's Florida.

you know you're in
florida when...
...you feel hot, reptilian breath on your neck

Gators occupy virtually every pond and waterway in the state, but it's not the real thing unless you pay an admission fee, right?

Seriously, Florida has many fun and/or educational gator-based attractions, ranging from kitschy mom-and-pop operations to major tourist destinations. Many also let you touch a real live alligator, which is not something we recommend you do to the 10-footer basking outside your motel room.

Here's a sampling of parks devoted to the gator.

St. Augustine Alligator Farm Zoological Park (St. Augustine; www .alligatorfarm.com): Opened in 1890, Alligator Farm is one of Florida's oldest tourist attractions. Over 1,000 gators and crocs are on display, including a 13-foot gator named Baby Huey and a rare albino gator.

Gatorland (Kissimmee; www.gatorland .com): Another venerable gator farm, opened in 1949. Home of the Gator Jumparoo Show, where chicken carcasses on a wire inspire mammoth gators to leap to unsettling heights.

Gatorama (Palmdale; www.gatorama.com): A venerable Florida roadside attraction with nearly 4,000 gators and crocs, about 60 of which are 12 feet or longer. After you watch the gators being fed, you can feed yourself some gator in the Gatorama restaurant. Gator ribs are a menu specialty. They don't taste anything like chicken, or so we're told.

Jungle Adventures (Christmas; www .jungleadventures.com): Jungle Adventures is all about ecotourism, which means it's more devoted to education that some of the other attractions. Besides alligators, there are black bears and a rare Florida panther. Gator meat and belts are available in the Gator Store.

Gator Attractions:

A sizeable segment of Florida's tourist industry is based on the ubiquitous gator. Makes sense to us.

you know you're in
florida when...
...you need a thirst quencher

Is it in you? If you are an imbiber of sports drinks, chances are good that it is.

Gatorade, the performance-enhancing beverage created at the University of Florida (UF), owns 80 to 90 percent of the sports-drink market. That's a lot of Extremo Tropico and Riptide Rush, to name just two of the many Gatorade flavors that have come out since the drink first hit grocery shelves in 1967.

Gatorade was created by UF researchers Dr. Robert Cade and Dr. Dana Shires in 1966 and named after the school's football team, the Gators. A Gator football coach had asked Dr. Cade why his players sometimes lost 20 pounds playing in the wilting Florida heat but never had the urge to urinate. The players were losing the weight through perspiration, of course, but Dr. Cade speculated that they were also losing significant amounts of sodium and potassium, electrolytes needed to maintain the body's delicate chemical balance and provide energy—something Gator players were sorely lacking in the second half of a game.

Dr. Cade used the freshman team as guinea pigs to test his theory. They were cooperative . . . up to a point. "They would not consent to having practice stopped so we could measure their body temperature rectally," he recalls.

The first batch of the test drink, which was not much more than water mixed with sugar and salt, tasted so vile that no one would drink it. Dr. Cade's wife suggested mixing in lemon juice, and the drink that would soon become known as Gatorade was born.

Dehydrated no longer, the Gators won their first Orange Bowl in 1967 and gained a reputation as a strong second-half team. Gatorade pitchman Michael Jordan added millions of dollars more to his towering pile of dough. And the University of Florida has received at least $80 million in royalties since 1973, money it has spent on a variety of research projects.

Not bad for what is essentially fortified water.

Gatorade:

This popular sports drink was invented on the University of Florida campus. Michael Jordan, on the other hand, was not.

you know you're in
florida when...
...you see Alice going to the moon

"From the sun and fun capital of the world, Miami Beach, it's the *Jackie Gleason Show!*"

On Saturday nights from 1966 to 1970, these words introduced the last variety show of the self-proclaimed "Great One," Jackie Gleason.

Gleason moved his production company (and home) to South Florida in 1964 from New York. With the help of the June Taylor Dancers, the show (not to be confused with the far-superior *Honeymooners* series of the 1950s) is credited with introducing to sleepy Miami Beach a showbiz glamour that eventually changed the face of the town.

In case you're wondering, after leaving the *Jackie Gleason Show* June Taylor became the choreographer for the Miami Dolphins cheerleaders. She died in Miami Beach in 2004 at the age of 86. Her sister, Marilyn Taylor Horwich Gleason, married Jackie Gleason in 1975 and remained his wife until his death in 1987 in Ft. Lauderdale.

The *Jackie Gleason Show* featured musical reenactments of the classic *Honeymooners* episodes. Although Art Carney, who played Norton in the original series, continued as Gleason's sidekick (and nemesis), the show was hurt by the absence of Audrey Meadows and Joyce Randolph, who played Alice and Trixie in the original.

The *Jackie Gleason Show:*

By staging this show in the Sun and Fun Capital of the World, the self-proclaimed "Great One" helped put Miami Beach on the map.

STAY TUNED FOR
THE HONEYMOONERS
STARRING
JACKIE GLEASON

Still, Gleason's gigantic (in more ways than one) stage presence won the show a wide audience, if little in the way of critical acclaim.

None of it seemed to matter to the laid-back Gleason, who concluded each show by taking sips of something from a coffee cup—something that no one believed to be coffee.

As the Great One would say: "And away we go!"

you know you're in
florida when...
... someone yells "FORE!"

It is no accident that Spaceship Earth at Epcot Center is shaped like a giant golf ball.

Golf is huge in Florida, which boasts 1,250 courses (and counting), more than any other state in the United States. The World Golf Hall of Fame, the PGA Tour, the Champions Tour, the LPGA, and the PGA of America are all headquartered in Florida. Five PGA Tour tournaments are played in Florida, including Arnold Palmer's Bay Hill Invitational in Orlando and the prestigious Tournament Players Championship (sometimes called "the fifth major") in Ponte Vedra.

You might think that it would be easier to play golf in pancake-flat Florida than in hillier locales. Not necessarily. Lots of dirt is needed to raise Florida courses out of the swamps, and the resulting holes become lakes. Lots and lots of lakes.

To make their courses more eye-appealing (or simply because they're sadists), Florida golf-course architects often build a lot of sand traps into their designs. Our personal rule of thumb is bunker, lake, lake, bunker, bunker, then put the ball in the pocket.

The high season for golf in Florida is January to March, the peak of tourist season. Greens fees skyrocket, and it's a good idea to schedule your tee time well ahead.

Golf:

With more golf courses than any other state, Florida is a favorite destination for those who like to chase the little white ball.

Summer is when the locals reclaim their courses (and their restaurants, and their beaches, and their roads, etc., etc.). Greens fees plummet, and lots of times you'll have the course all to yourself. That is, if you don't mind the heat, humidity, bugs, and thunderstorms that seem to spring up between 3:00 and 4:00 P.M. every day like clockwork.

Hey, that's the price you pay for living in Golf Heaven.

you know you're in
florida when...
...you're visiting Papa's house

Perhaps no American author is connected to a place more than Ernest Hemingway is to Key West. Hemingway lived on the island from 1928 to 1940 and produced some of his best writing here, including the final drafts of *A Farewell to Arms* and *The Snows of Kilimanjaro*.

But most tourists don't visit the Hemingway House and Museum (907 Whitehead Street, Old Town Key West; admission charged) to pay homage to the author's terse prose. The come to see the weird cats.

The grounds of the home on Whitehead Street are overrun by more than 60 six-toed cats. (Some of the cats even have seven toes, but once you get to six, most people stop counting.) The original multidigit cats were said to have been given to Hemingway by a sea captain. For reasons known only to Hemingway, they had names like Bette Davis, Frank Sinatra, and Marilyn Monroe.

The House and Museum guides tell a lot of interesting stories about Hemingway. Some may even be true, such as the tale about the temper tantrum he threw when he learned the cost of a saltwater swimming pool built in his backyard.

For a more boisterous celebration of the Hemingway legend, you may want to attend Hemingway Days in July. The highlight of the weeklong festival is the Hemingway Look-Alike Contest, in which 150 or more burly, bearded men vie for the honor of being "Papa" for a year. Winner and losers all end up at Sloppy Joe's bar, a Duval Street watering hole that was Hemingway's favorite hangout. If you want to know how it feels to be Hemingway passed out on a barroom floor, order a Hemingway Hammer, which consists of 151-proof rum, banana and strawberry liquors, blackberry brandy, and a splash of white rum.

Our guess is that when the sun also rises, you'll wish it hadn't.

Ernest Hemingway:

The larger-than-life author worked and played in Key West. He also spent a lot of time in saloons.

you know you're in
florida when...
... you can recall the Big One

The so-called Labor Day hurricane of 1935 has the dubious distinction of being the most violent storm in American history.

With sustained winds of 200 mph and gusts possibly exceeding 250 mph (exact numbers are unavailable because all wind-measuring equipment was destroyed), the hurricane killed 423 people in the Keys: 164 civilians and 259 World War I veterans staying in work camps while building U.S. Highway 1. Most victims drowned when an 18-foot wall of water surged over the low-lying Keys. Some were killed by flying debris; some were simply sandblasted to death.

A memorial to them is located on Islamorada Key at mile marker 81.5, across from the library. Part of the memorial is a crypt that contains the bones and cremated remains of about 190 storm victims.

The coral rock–covered obelisk, officially called the Florida Keys Memorial, stands 18 feet tall and features a carved design of a giant wave and palm trees bending from a

Hurricane Memorial:

In the Keys there is a monument to those who perished in the most violent storm in American history.

DEDICATED

TO THE MEMORY OF THE
CIVILIANS AND WAR VETERANS
WHOSE LIVES WERE LOST
IN THE HURRICANE
OF SEPTEMBER 1935

terrific wind. The monument was built by the Works Progress Administration in 1937, two years after the devastating storm that is remembered to this day as the worst in Florida's history.

Charley, Frances, Ivan, and Jeanne. A regular Saturday-morning foursome? Hardly. Those are the names of four powerful hurricanes that lashed Florida during six awful weeks in 2004.

Though 2004 was exceptionally busy, hurricanes whack Florida more than any other state every year. Damage and loss of life can be extensive, but it is possible to overreact. When the September 16–17 hurricane of 1928 flattened West Palm Beach and caused the destructive Great Okeechobee Flood, a newspaper up north ran this excited headline: "Florida Is Destroyed! Florida Is Destroyed!"

If you live in Florida, you learn to deal with hurricanes. During the "season," which runs from June 1 to November 30, residents play closer attention to weather reports than they would otherwise. They make sure they have plenty of fresh batteries, a working radio, bottled water, and canned goods. They learn how to board up their windows and don't think it the least bit odd to throw their patio furniture into the pool when the winds pick up. When the power goes out, as it inevitably does, they rediscover the joys of card and board games. You are not a Floridian unless you've played at least one game of Monopoly by candlelight.

When it starts getting nasty, Floridians retreat to the "safe place" in their homes. That is a place (usually a hallway) that is far away from windows and can be sealed off from flying debris.

People who live on barrier islands or in other coastal areas are often ordered to evacuate when a hurricane approaches. This means a few nights sleeping on the floor of the local high school gymnasium.

A hurricane experience ranges from the mildly inconvenient to the downright terrifying, depending on how close the thing gets to you. The difference between losing a few branches from your trees and having your roof blow off is often a matter of just a few miles.

Every year Floridians gamble that they won't be hit by a hurricane. In 2004 many rolled the dice and lost.

Hurricanes:

These big storms are a fact of life in Florida, but in 2004 nature got a little carried away.

you know you're in
florida when...
...you've got your eye on the bouncing ball

It's called the fastest ball game in the world, which is odd because some of its best players tend to be on the chubby side.

But when the rock-hard jai alai ball (called a *pelota)* comes flying at you at 150 mph, waistline issues are the least of your concerns.

Jai alai (pronounced "HIGH-lie") originated centuries ago in the Basque region of northern Spain, where it was played outdoors using church walls as courts. The game came to Cuba in the late 19th century and then to the United States in 1926, when the Miami *fronton* (stadium) opened. Today, there are five frontons in Florida. (The Ft. Pierce fronton was badly damaged by the multiple hurricanes of 2004 and may or may not reopen.)

Jai alai is kind of a turbo-charged version of handball. It's played on a long, narrow court walled in on three sides. The pelota is caught and flung with a *cesta,* a long, curved wicker basket that is strapped to the player's hand. It is the whipping of the cesta that generates the tremendous ball speed.

In Basque, jai alai means "merry festival," which it certainly can be if you happen to place your bets on the winning player or team. Betting is done in a round-robin fash-

Jai Alai:

The fastest ball game in the world came to Florida from the Basque region of Spain. Today it's one of the more unusual ways to lose your money.

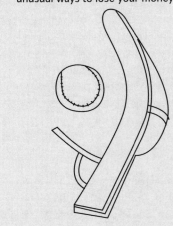

ion, so even if your pick loses a game or two, he or she still has a chance of winning the match.

We, unfortunately, have never had much luck choosing winners. What's the Basque word for "losing festival"?

you know you're in
florida when...
...you eat at Joe's

If it's a relaxing, romantic evening you're looking for, Joe's Stone Crab restaurant is probably not the place for you.

The atmosphere at Joe's, a Miami Beach institution since 1913, can best be described as ... pandemonium. The eatery's 400 seats are always full during stone crab season (October 15–May 15), and the wait for a table can sometimes be two hours. Or more. No reservations are accepted at Joe's; you line up with everyone else and wait your turn.

But if you love stone crab claws, the wait is worth it. The hard-shelled claws come pre-cracked, so all you have to do is dip them into Joe's equally famous mustard sauce and enjoy. Steaks and other seafood dishes are available, but if you're not coming to Joe's for stone crab claws, it hardly seems worth the bother.

Joe Weiss, a Hungarian immigrant, started Joe's as a lunch stand next to Smith's bathing casino. Joe's specialty was fish sandwiches until a local ichthyologist urged him to boil up some stone crabs, a prevalent but widely ignored denizen of the local bays. The claws (the only edible part of the crab) were an instant hit, and Joe's restaurant soon became a local landmark. Over the years, everyone who is anyone has dined at Joe's: Al Capone, Will Rogers, Amelia Earhart, the Duke and Duchess of Windsor, and J. Edgar Hoover (presumably

not while Scarface was in the building). More recently, former President Bill Clinton dined at Joe's. (He reportedly ordered the fried chicken.)

Taking up an entire city block, Joe's is located in the heart of Miami Beach's flamboyant nightclub district (11 Washington Avenue; 305–673–0365; www.joesstone crab.com). So between bites of stone crab, you can occupy your time with people-watching.

Dinner at Joe's is pretty much a must for anyone visiting south Florida for the first time. But don't go if you're in a hurry; restaurants over 90 years old are entitled to move at their own pace.

Joe's Stone Crab:

The most popular entree at this Miami Beach institution is—you guessed it—stone crab claws. Bring your credit card and pass the melted butter.

45

you know you're in
florida when...
...you spot a tiny deer

Bambi is alive and well and living on Big Pine Key.

The pine forests of this largely undeveloped island are home to North America's smallest deer. Looking more like a medium-size dog than a deer, an adult Key deer might weigh only 45 pounds and stand only 25 inches tall at the shoulder.

Needless to say, these little guys are adorably cute, to the point that you just want to scoop one up in your arms and take him home with you. That, of course, would be a big mistake. Key deer are a protected species; take all the photos you want, but don't try to feed them, pet them, or cuddle them.

Almost all of the Key deer in the world live in Monroe County. They're the diminutive cousins of the Virginia white-tailed deer and are believed to have become stranded on the Keys thousands of years ago when rising water cut off their access to the mainland.

Once hunted with dogs nearly to the point of extinction, Key deer now number in the 250 to 300 range. Stray dogs still kill a few of these critters every year. Loss of habitat and traffic on busy U.S. Highway 1 are also threats.

The best place to see a Key deer is at the National Key Deer Refuge on Big Pine Key. (If that's too far a drive, try Lowry Park Zoo in Tampa; it has a few Key deer on display.) The fawn-colored animals are most active in the morning and evening, but chances are good that you'll see one at any time of day.

It's like watching a Disney animated feature, only without the popcorn.

Key Deer:

This diminutive species exists only in south Florida.

you know you're in
florida when...
...you make Key lime pie

On first sight—or bite—the Key lime is unlikely to bowl you over.

Unlike the larger Persian lime, its skin is mottled yellow, not shiny green. It's seedy and small, not much bigger than a walnut. And, most distinctively, its taste is puckeringly sour. So why all the fuss about a gnarly little lime that makes your face turn inside out? Three words: Key lime pie.

The official dessert of Key West, Key lime pie is described by *A Gourmet's Guide* as "an American pie containing a lime-flavored custard topped with meringue." This is incredibly simplistic; the question of whipped cream vs. meringue—let alone the correct composition of a graham-cracker crust—can get you into a Duval Street bar fight.

Key limes were the standard of the world before Persian limes and other varieties came along. Aside from their other drawbacks (see above), Key limes are sensitive to cold and grow on thorny trees. But if you lived in a tropical climate, wanted a good source of vitamin C, and weren't afraid of pricked fingers, Key limes got the job done.

Key limes were grown commercially in southern Florida and the Keys until a 1926 hurricane wiped out the groves. Small-scale and backyard production continues, however, so it is still possible to find the main ingredient of Key lime pie locally. (Do not

use bottled Key lime juice if you can avoid it. The taste is nothing like that of the real, fresh-squeezed thing.)

Key lime pie became identified with Key West because of the island's isolation. Before the Florida East Coast Railroad opened in 1912, fresh milk was hard to come by. Gail Borden's invention of sweetened condensed (canned) milk in 1859 solved the problem: It allowed you to make a custard pie without cooking it. The Key lime juice was so sour that it curdled the milk and egg yolks, creating an instant filling. (Today's concerns about salmonella usually result in the pie being baked to an internal temperature of 160 degrees.)

If you wish to accompany your slice of Key lime pie with a cold glass of sweet iced tea, you will not offend us.

Key Lime Pie:

The fruit that's used in this dessert is barely bigger than a Ping-Pong ball, but the taste will have you bouncing back for more.

you know you're in
florida when...
...keys aren't martyrs

Why are the Florida Keys called the Keys?

Don't blame Ponce de Leon, he of Fountain of Youth fame. The explorer, who apparently suffered from a much-too-vivid imagination (perhaps brought on by too much sun), decided after first seeing the chain of islands at Florida's tip that they looked like men who were suffering. (Remember, this was way before wives started dragging their husbands off to souvenir shops.) He gave the islands the name Los Marteres, or "the martyrs."

Perhaps residents realized that future chambers of commerce might have trouble warming up to the slogan "Be a Martyr! Visit Martyr West!" In any case, the chain was eventually renamed the Keys, from the Spanish *cayos*, meaning "small islands."

So today we have Key Largo and Marathon Key and Big Pine Key, but no Martyr Key. Which is probably a good thing.

The Keys:

The name for these islands has nothing to do with those things that unlock doors.

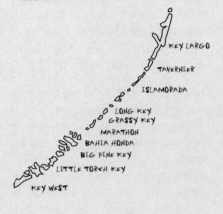

Whether the movie *The Invasion of the Body Snatchers* was inspired by kudzu is a question we'll leave to film historians.

All we know is that kudzu—also known, less flatteringly, as cuss you, the foot-a-night vine, and the Vine That Ate the South—is more abundant in the South than barbecue and far less popular. The aggressive vine covers seven million acres in the Deep South and would surely cover more if people weren't working so hard to get rid of the stuff.

Kudzu did not always have such a bad reputation. You could say it grew into it. The oriental vine was first introduced to this country in 1876, when the Japanese used it to shade their exhibit booth at the U.S. Centennial Exposition in Philadelphia. The idea caught on, and soon people from Virginia to Alabama were planting the stuff as a porch vine.

Enter Charles E. and Lillie Pleas, a kindly Quaker couple who had relocated from Indiana to tiny Chipley in northwest Florida. Both naturalists, the Pleas discovered that animals would eat the plant, so they began promoting its use as forage in the 1920s. Their Glen Arden Nursery sold kudzu plants through the mail. A historical marker on the site of the old nursery, now the Washington County Agricultural Center on U.S. Highway 90, proudly proclaims "Kudzu Developed Here."

Kudzu:

A pair of Florida horticulturists have the dubious distinction of being the people who popularized the Vine That Ate the South.

During the Great Depression of the 1930s, the Soil Conservation Service promoted kudzu for erosion control. (Its very ability to hold soil in place is what makes it so hard to kill; kudzu's roots can extend 8 feet into the earth.)

The problem with kudzu is that it grows too well, smothering native crops and plants and covering trees so densely that they die for lack of light. The vine can grow as quickly as a foot a day, and some herbicides actually make it grow faster.

Today all that remains of the Pleas' (dubious) contribution to horticultural history is the commemorative marker and the couple's side-by-side graves in Glenwood Cemetery on Glenwood Avenue. Their vine-free tombstone reads, simply, "Kudzu Pioneers."

49

you know you're in
florida when...
...you're on the banks of a really big lake

Lake Okeechobee is enormous—it's the second largest lake in America behind Lake Superior—but you can't see it from the road.

The three-story-high Herbert Hoover Dike surrounds Lake Okeechobee for 140 miles, obstructing the views. The dike was built in the early 1930s, after the big hurricane of 1928 flooded the lake and killed at least 2,500 people.

Controlling the waters of the lake, which cover 730 square miles but average only 10 feet deep, has been a priority ever since. Today Lake Okeechobee is essentially a giant reservoir. A series of locks, dikes, and canals provides irrigation to a $1.5 billion agricultural industry (sugar cane, winter vegetables, and rice are the main crops) and drinking water to six million people, mostly in the southeastern part of the state.

In the old days, before the Army Corps of Engineers got involved, Lake Okeechobee was the spigot for the giant swamp that is the Everglades. During the summer rainy season, the shallow lake would spill its banks and flow ever so slowly south to Florida Bay, nourishing the saw grass and the Everglades' abundant wildlife. In the winter the water stopped flowing and the 'Glades dried up.

Lake Okeechobee doesn't look like it used to, but it's still a top fishing destination.

Lake Okeechobee:

The Seminole word for "big water" is also Florida's largest lake and a bit player in the Everglades' ecology.

Anglers flock to the self-proclaimed Bass Capital of the World, hoping to hook up with one of the legendary lunkers that lurk in the lake's tannic waters.

If fishing isn't your thing, you can hike or bicycle atop the Hoover Dike, now part of the Florida National Scenic Trail. Or you can visit one of the nearby Seminole-run casinos. You can even sing a few stanzas of "Way Down Upon the Okeechobee" if you wish. But you'll have to make up your own lyrics.

Floridians love their warm weather, their beaches, and their abundant wildlife.

But oddly enough, they also have a soft spot for license plates. While the most common license plate image continues to be the giant orange superimposed on a silhouette of the state, at last count there were 88 specialty—or, if you prefer, "vanity"—plates decorating the rear bumpers of Florida's cars, vans, and trucks.

By shelling out an additional $15 to $25 at registration time, you can express your support of a variety of environmental causes (manatees, coral reefs, panthers); professional sports teams (Tampa Bay Devil Rays, Miami Dolphins, Jacksonville Jaguars); universities/colleges (Ringling School of Art and Design, Embry-Riddle Aeronautical University, University of Florida); causes (End Breast Cancer, Florida Arts, Florida Special Olympics); hobbies/occupations (Golf Capital of the World, Motorcycles, Agriculture); or military service (U.S. Army, U.S. Air Force, U.S. Coast Guard).

There is a severe popularity gap among the 88 plates. The most requested plate, Save the Panthers, was bought or renewed by 100,585 drivers in 2003, whereas the Nova Southeastern University plate found only four takers.

Some of the plates are relatively straightforward, while others qualify as genuine works of art. (The Everglades River of Grass plate, featuring a roseate spoonbill against a setting sun, is our personal favorite, with the exuberantly colorful State Wildflower a close second.)

Specialty plate fees have raised millions of dollars for their various groups or causes, so it seems safe to say that even more specialty plates will be forthcoming.

Can the Protect the Sandspur or Save the Fire Ant plate be far behind?

License Plates:

Who needs bumper stickers? No matter what team you like or which cause you support, Florida has a license plate for you.

you know you're in
florida when...
...you're glowing in the dark

Florida has the dubious distinction of being the Lightning Capital of the World. The state's hot, moist summers and situation between the Gulf of Mexico and Atlantic Ocean result in an average of 12 strikes per square kilometer per year, according to the U.S. National Weather Service.

Lightning is the second-leading cause of weather-related deaths in the United States, behind floods. (Florida has floods, too, as well as hurricanes, tornadoes, and senior citizens driving slow in the left-hand lane. We're not afraid of saying any of this because if four hurricanes in six weeks don't scare tourists away, nothing will.)

More lightning deaths occur in Florida than any other state. (Only Alaskans don't have to worry about lightning, but then again, few if any Floridians have ever been gored by a moose.) The reason, besides the conducive climate, is that Floridians spend a lot of time outside doing lightning-daring activities like golfing and boating.

Remember, lighting likes to go for the tallest thing around. Professional golfer Lee Trevino said that even God can't hit a one iron, but we don't recommend waving one over your head when the sky turns dark.

Here are some lightning "fun" facts: (1) One bolt of lightning can keep a 100-watt light bulb lit for three months. Personally, we feel safer fulfilling our electrical needs through Florida Power and Light. (2) A cloud-to-ground lightning bolt heats the air around it to 50,000 degrees Fahrenheit, hotter than the surface of the sun. For you picnickers, that kind of heat will definitely char your wieners. The scorching heat causes the air around the bolt to expand violently, creating the explosion known as thunder.

A rule of thumb for lightning safety: When you see lightning, begin counting. If you hear thunder before you get to 30, seek shelter immediately. Then wait at least 30 minutes after the last rumble to resume your activities.

Lightning:

Florida has the dubious distinction of being the Lightning Capital of the World, but there are things you can do to lessen your chance of being struck.

you know you're in
florida when...
...you're touring the southern White House

President Harry S. Truman so loved the Little White House in Key West that he referred to his other place in Washington, D.C., as "The Great White Jail."

While president, Truman made 10 visits to the Little White House, which previously had been the Navy base's commandant's quarters. Truman took full advantage of Key West's laid-back atmosphere to relax and unwind. Inside the museum (111 Front Street; 305–294–9911; admission charged) you'll see pictures of the 33rd president in his "Key West uniform," typically a floral Hawaiian shirt. Perhaps taking a clue from fellow Key Wester Ernest Hemingway, Truman liked to start his day early with a shot of bourbon and a chaser of orange juice.

The 10-room house/museum contains many Truman artifacts, including the original piano and poker table (both of which saw much use) and a framed copy of the front page of the *Chicago Tribune* with the infamous headline "Dewey Beats Truman."

Subsequent presidents also made use of the Little White House. President Eisenhower visited in 1956 to recuperate from a heart attack. President Kennedy and Great Britain Prime Minister Harold Macmillan held a one-day summit there in 1961, and

Little White House:

Harry S. Truman loved his home away from home so much that he didn't want to go back to Washington, D.C. Can't say that we blame him.

President Carter and his family held a reunion there in 1996.

But it was Truman who truly thought of the place as home. In fact, he once wrote a letter to his wife, Bess, confessing that if was up to him, he'd move the capital of the United States from Washington, D.C., to Key West.

Who knows? It might do our presidents good to spend more time in Hawaiian shirts.

You don't have to offer an in-flight dinner and movie to get love bugs to fly United. It's definitely what these harmless black flies do best.

If you drive through Florida in May or September, you are sure to have a close encounter of the windshield kind with these shameless practitioners of aerial amour. The bane of motorists and the boon of car washes, love bugs do not sting or bite or carry any diseases. They just hook up with each other, end to end (preferably over highways; they're turned on by auto exhaust), until the smaller male drops dead from exhaustion (or carbon monoxide poisoning) or the tandem splats against a windshield, whichever comes first. Life can be precarious when you're madly in love. (See *Romeo and Juliet*.)

Your average Floridian is much more familiar with love bugs than he is with swamp cabbage or manatees or conchs, so it was just a matter of time before somebody came up with the idea of a Love Bug Festival. That man is Ted Eubanks, and his celebration of the bug of love takes place the first weekend of June at the fairgrounds in Marianna. There is the usual assortment of arts and crafts, food vendors, and sack races, but the highlight of the festival is the crowning of Little Miss Love Bug.

We asked Ted if Little Miss Love Bug celebrates her victory by killing Little Mister Love Bug or pasting herself on the windshield of a passing Ford Explorer. Happily (or sadly, depending on how sick you are), Little Miss Love Bug does neither. She simply thanks the judges and then moseys off for a funnel cake and maybe some ribs.

Ted says he hopes to add more love-buggy elements to future festivals, including a costume parade. "About all we have now is a 2-inch-by-2-inch love bug house," he says. "Love bugs could fly in there if they wanted to, but so far they haven't."

Marianna is located about 60 miles northwest of Tallahassee off U.S. Highway 90. For more information, call (850) 526–7777.

Love Bugs:

Though they don't bite or sting, these amorous black flies have never met a car radiator they didn't like.

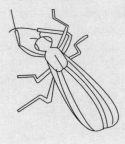

you know you're in
florida when...
...you're reading a Travis McGee novel

"I've always recognized that Florida is a slightly tacky state. You love it in spite of itself."

John D. MacDonald, the speaker of those words, detailed his conflicted affection for his adopted state (he was born in Pennsylvania) during a 40-year writing career that produced more than 100 novels. After MacDonald moved to Siesta Key, near Sarasota, in 1949, his work dealt almost exclusively with Florida. The state's ecological dangers, racism, political corruption, real estate scams, and drug deals all became fodder for the prolific novelist.

MacDonald, who died in 1986, is probably best remembered as the creator of Travis McGee, the most "colorful" of unlicensed private detectives. (All 21 of the Travis McGee novels have a color in their title.)

The fictional McGee, whom MacDonald described as "a tattered knight on a spavined steed," lived in Ft. Lauderdale aboard a houseboat named *The Busted Flush*—after the poker hand that won it for him.

There is a lot of MacDonald in Travis McGee, but the two are not carbon copies. McGee was catnip to the ladies, while MacDonald was married to the same woman for more than 50 years. But McGee,

John D. MacDonald:

This creator of a quirky detective series had a deep and abiding love of Florida.

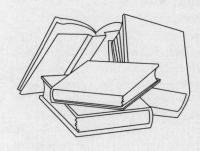

like MacDonald, saw himself as a champion of justice in a world with far too little of it.

The first Travis McGee novel, *The Deep Blue Goodbye,* was published in 1964. It's a good idea to read the novels in the order in which they were published, but if you have time to read only one or two, we recommend *A Dreadful Lemon Sky* and *The Green Ripper.*

you know you're in
florida when...
...you know a manatee from a mermaid

In Christopher Columbus's era, sailors who had been at sea a long time sometimes confused manatees with mermaids, the sexy half-fish, half-women of nautical legend.

All we can say about this is that anyone who would mistake a whiskered, 1,200-pound West Indian manatee with Daryl Hannah of the 1984 movie *Splash* has either been out in the sun far too long or dipped a little too heavily into the grog, or both.

The manatee's nickname is "sea cow," which should tell you all you need to know about its lissome physique. Fortunately, manatees have other things going for them, like a gentle personality. You can swim with them, touch them, even feed them if the two of you are in the right mood. No mermaid, to our knowledge, would permit such familiarities.

Furthermore, manatees are endangered, which means that legions of environmentalists have taken up the cause of protecting these docile giants. Since most of the state's 2,000 to 3,000 manatees live in warm waters close to shore, the slow-moving animals are constantly getting run over by boats, tied up in fishing line, or otherwise tormented by people. Boat run-ins are so common that wildlife officials have learned to identify manatees by the propeller scars on their backs.

The Save the Manatee Club (www.savethemanatee.org) is a good place to learn more about these unusual marine mammals, which are more closely related to elephants than they are to cows.

Visit the spring-fed Crystal River about two hours west of Orlando if you want to meet a manatee face-to-face. Snorkeling and scuba-diving expeditions can be arranged through one of several outfitters operating along this clear, 72-degree river.

The less adventurous can visit Snooty at downtown Bradenton's Parker Aquarium (201 Tenth Street; 941–746–4131). At 56, Snooty is the oldest living manatee in captivity. Try to arrive at feeding time; it's a cute spectacle. Not mermaid-cute, but cute.

Manatees:

Anyone who would confuse these blubbery gray mammals with mermaids needs to seriously cut back on his rum intake.

florida when...

...rafts are a ride to freedom

In the spring of 1980, Fidel Castro emptied some of Cuba's prisons and asylums and sent the inmates to Florida in what became known as the Mariel Boatlift. (Mariel Harbor was the point of debarkation.)

When Castro opened the port to all Cuban citizens, many impoverished freedom seekers fled his Communist dictatorship, hoping to find work in America. Over a period of six months, they crammed aboard about 1,700 mostly unseaworthy boats, some hardly more than rafts. Approximately 125,000 refugees survived the 90-mile passage across the turbulent Florida Straits; most of them landed in Miami. Although the U.S. Coast Guard provided massive assistance, it was overwhelmed by the size of the exodus. By the time the boatlift ended in October, 27 refugees had died, 14 of them on one overloaded vessel.

Upon arrival many Cubans went to refugee camps, although some dangerous criminals were placed in federal prisons to await deportation. In time many of the refugees, who called themselves "Marielitos," blended into the Miami community, which already had a sizeable Cuban population.

Public outcry over the "fast one" that Fidel Castro had apparently pulled on America was one of the factors leading to President Jimmy Carter's defeat when he ran for reelection in 1980.

Mariel Boatlift:

This historic 1980 event saw 125,000 Cubans leave the port of Mariel for Florida, with most settling in Miami.

The beginning of the classic 1983 movie *Scarface* recalls the Mariel Boatlift. Tony Montana, played by Al Pacino, says that he has fled Cuba to seek the American Dream. It ends up being a very twisted dream involving lots of guns and cocaine, but it's about what you'd expect from a guy who had the same nickname as Al Capone.

In the 1980s Miami was America's biggest port of entry for cocaine from Colombia, Bolivia, and Peru. Billions of dollars of drug money brought luxury car dealerships, five-star hotels, swanky nightclubs, and other forms of prosperity. But it also spawned a violent crime wave that lasted well into the 1990s.

How do you deal with a problem like this? Why, you create a hit TV cop show, of course. *Miami Vice,* which ran from 1984 to 1989 on NBC, made undercover police work seem cool. Detective Sonny Crockett (played by Don Johnson) drove around in a white Ferrari and had a pet alligator named Elvis. He and his partner, Detective Ricardo Tubbs (played by Philip Michael Thomas), careened around a Miami that existed only in a scriptwriter's imagination, pursuing drug dealers, gun runners, bad cops, and really hot women.

Everything about this show had style. Executive producer Michael Mann was inspired to create the show's trademark pastel color scheme after a visit to a paint store. America soon fell in love with pastels, from fashion to interior decor.

Miami Vice also had terrific music. In fact, the soundtrack is the most successful TV soundtrack of all time. (Second place belongs to Henry Mancini's music from *Peter Gunn.*)

Miami Vice:

This hit TV show from the 1980s captured the danger and color of south Florida's drug culture.

There were sunsets and palm trees, cigarette boats and car chases, and lots and lots of cool guns. (Cool if you like guns, of course. Which we do, but only in the context of a cop show.)

As of this writing, Crockett's white Ferrari Testarossa was on display at the Swap Shop Flea Market in Sunrise. Is this a great country, or what?

you know you're in
florida when...
...you're catching a buzz

If you love mosquitoes—and who doesn't?—then Flamingo is the place for you.

Located at the southern tip of Florida, Flamingo, population 65 and itching, is hidden deep within Everglades National Park. You do not stumble upon Flamingo; you must want to get there very much.

Connected to the rest of the state by a 50-mile park road, Flamingo probably has more mosquitoes per cubic inch of air than any other place in Florida, if not the world. It is the home of the aggressive black salt marsh mosquito. These little buggers attack in clouds of up to 500 a minute, flying into your ears and up your nose. If you try to talk or open your mouth to breathe, you will probably swallow dozens of them.

Of course, you don't have to go all the way to Flamingo to get bitten. Florida's warm, wet climate is ideal for mosquito breeding, which, unfortunately, can lead to mosquito-borne diseases such as malaria and dengue fever (both very rare now in the U.S.) and more troublesome afflictions such as West Nile virus, St. Louis encephalitis, and eastern equine encephalitis. Dog heartworm is also caused by mosquito bites.

There are 75 species of mosquitoes in Florida, some with fun-sounding names like "feather legged gallinipper" and "white socks." There's nothing funny about the main disease-carrying mosquito in Florida,

Culex nigripalpus, the bug responsible for encephalitis.

Here are some mosquito "fun" facts: (1) Mosquitoes lay their eggs in stagnant water. The water collecting in that used tire in your backyard will never be useful, so dump it. (2) Only female mosquitoes suck blood. Male mosquitoes drink nectar from flowers. So much for females being the gentler sex. (3) After the eggs hatch, mosquitoes can be up and biting in less than four days. Mosquito parents don't have to worry about setting money aside for college. (4) Insect repellants containing DEET work better than anything else. Suits of armor are also effective.

Try to avoid going outside during early morning and early evening hours, when mosquitoes are most active. If you must go outside, move very quickly.

Mosquitoes:

These biting insects can live just about anywhere, but the small south Florida village of Flamingo is Mosquito Heaven.

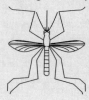

you know you're in
florida when...
...movies are a major industry

Yes, it's true that *Revenge of the Nerds 2* was filmed in Ft. Lauderdale in 1987, but we'd like to just forget about that if it's OK with you.

Florida's film industry began about the same time as film itself. Florida's first "movie" was an 1898 newsreel of U.S. troops in Tampa during the Spanish-American War.

Before World War I, Jacksonville boasted 30 studios and 1,000 actors and extras. By 1995 Florida was the third largest filmmaking state in the country, having successfully lured such major studios as Universal, Disney, and MGM to establish Florida offices.

Here is a sampling of movies that have been made (at least in part) in Florida:

Moon Over Miami (1941) was filmed in Miami and at Cypress Gardens in Winter Haven.

Twelve O'Clock High (1949) was filmed at Eglin Air Force Base.

The Greatest Show on Earth (1952) was filmed at Barnum and Bailey headquarters in Sarasota.

Creature from the Black Lagoon (1954) was filmed in 3-D at Wakulla Springs and Tarpon Springs.

Select scenes in *Goldfinger* (1964) were filmed at the Fontainebleau Hotel in Miami.

Select scenes in **The Godfather: Part II** (1974) were filmed in Miami.

Jaws 2 (1978) was filmed at Gulf Islands National Seashore and Navarre Beach.

Porky's (1981) was filmed in Miami. OK, this movie was really stupid, but you have to admit that the scene with the hole in the shower wall was pretty funny. (Or maybe you don't.)

Cocoon (1985) was filmed in St. Petersburg and Clearwater.

Select scenes in **Apollo 13** (1995) were filmed at Kennedy Space Center.

Sunshine State (2002) was filmed on Amelia Island, and **Monster** (2003) was filmed in six Florida locations.

Movies:

Florida was there at the beginning of the film age and continues to produce great works to this day, such as *Revenge of the Nerds 2.*

you know you're in
florida when...
... people sell fish by the highway

You cannot consider yourself a real Floridian until you have dug your fingers into a slab of smoked mullet.

It's a common sight in Florida to see an orthodontically challenged individual smoking mullet in a converted oil drum alongside the road. You smell the smoke or spot the crudely lettered sign, pull off onto the shoulder, and pay the guy around $3.00 for a warm, split, freshly smoked fish that is so heavenly fragrant that you usually start digging into it before you make it back home.

The black mullet is not the official state fish (that honor goes to sailfish and largemouth bass), but it should be. Florida produces more than 75 percent of the country's mullet, and down here it is considered a delicacy, best served fried or smoked.

Mullet are bottom-dwelling fish that congregate in large schools. They average two to three pounds apiece and often give themselves away by repeatedly leaping into the air and loudly smacking back down into the water. Overfishing resulted in a commercial netting ban in 1995, but you can still catch mullet the old-fashioned way by pitching a castnet off a low bridge. (Be advised that this particular skill requires considerable practice.)

There are not one, but two, mullet celebrations in Florida. The Boggy Bayou Mullet Festival takes place in Niceville, in the Pan-

Mullet:

Whether it's served up smoked or deep fried, this tasty fish is a favorite of Floridians.

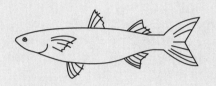

handle, on the third weekend in October. According to the festival's Web site (www.mulletfestival.com), the food includes "mullet, fried gator tail and other stuff Yankees don't normally eat." Family fun includes "clowns, ponies, snakes, and stuff."

The other mullet-related event is the Interstate Mullet Toss in Pensacola on the last full weekend in April. Contestants line up on the Gulf of Mexico beach just across the state line in Alabama and toss a mullet back into Florida. (Beer is an essential ingredient of a successful mullet toss.)

Before you animal-rights activists start writing letters, be advised that no live mullet are used in this event.

you know you're in
florida when...
...you can't see what's biting you

No-see-ums are sometimes called sand flies or "punkies." We usually refer to them as "flying jaws."

As their name implies, no-see-ums are exceedingly small. They pass through your average window screen the way a car passes through a tunnel. Worse yet, insect repellants have little effect on these voracious little monsters. What, you thought Florida was one big Disney World?

No-see-ums operate much like mosquitoes. They're blood-suckers; the dirty work is done entirely by the females; and they're most active at dusk and dawn. The flies, technically a kind of biting midge, breed in pooling water or moist vegetation. They're especially happy in coastal areas, making an evening clambake on the beach a very slap-happy proposition.

The bite of the no-see-um is entirely disproportionate to its size. Mosquitoes are gentle by comparison, and when you smack them, at least you know you've hit something.

The best defense against no-see-ums is to stay indoors when they're most active. (If you're having an evening cocktail party on the lanai, a strong fan will usually dissuade them, but it's hard keeping the napkins in place.)

No-see-ums:

You can't see them, but when they bite you, you definitely know they're there.

Believe it or not, there are two positive things we can say about no-see-ums. First, they are not dangerous carriers of disease like mosquitoes. Second, freshwater fish love to eat them, meaning that when the swarms are at their thickest, you should reach for your fishing pole.

Please try to remember these happy facts as you're applying ice to your welts.

you know you're in
florida when...
...you seem to have misplaced your clothes

With its warm climate and abundant sunshine, Florida is a great place to come to if you want to . . . get naked.

If should come as no surprise that Florida has more nudist resorts and nude beaches than any other state. (Nudists, by the way, refer to vacation spots where clothes are worn as "textile resorts.")

For some reason, the Tampa Bay area is especially thick with nudist resorts. Five of the state's 14 resorts are located here, including the Lake Como Family Nudist Resort in Land O' Lakes, site of the Super Bowl South Volleyball Tournament every March.

In business since 1947, Lake Como is the oldest nudist resort in the state. Its clientele is mostly couples and families, and activities include swimming, tennis, volleyball, pentanque (a kind of paddle ball), boating, and sunning, of course. In the evenings, everyone heads down to the lakeside bar, otherwise known as the Butt Hutt.

Experienced nudists say that if you're new to the nude-recreation experience, you might want to try a nudist resort before going to a nude beach. (More shade, for one thing.)

For more information on Florida's nudist resorts, visit the Web site for the American Association for Nude Recreation: www.aanr.com. (A playful lot, members sometimes like to abbreviate their organization's name to American Ass. for Nude Recreation.)

If you decide to visit one of Florida's nudist resorts, remember one thing: Bring lots of sunscreen.

Nudist Resorts:

The warm climate and abundant sunshine make Florida a great place to lose your clothes . . . and your inhibitions.

you know you're in
florida when...
... you feel you've been transported to Arabia

Entering the city of Opa-Locka in northern Miami-Dade County is like stepping through the pages of *The Arabian Nights*.

The entire city, founded in 1926, is done up in a Moorish theme. Everywhere you turn you'll see domes, parapets, minarets, and keyhole arches. City Hall, located on Sharazad Boulevard, looks like an elaborate Persian palace. With more than 80 themed buildings still standing, Opa-Locka claims the largest collection of Moorish architecture in the Western Hemisphere. Twenty of the buildings are on the National Register of Historic Places.

Opa-Locka was the brainchild of Glen H. Curtiss, a brilliant engineer and inventor from New York. (Curtiss is quite a story himself. He was featured on the cover of *Time* magazine in 1924 and has been declared the Father of Naval Aviation.) Like many others, Curtiss came to Florida in the 1920s to speculate in real estate. He wound up founding several south Florida cities, including Hialeah, Miami Springs, and Coral Gables.

But it's Opa-Locka that causes people to stop, scratch their heads, and go, "Huh?"

Apparently, Curtiss was just ga-ga over the book *The Arabian Nights*, especially the descriptions of the ornate architecture. So he thought he'd build a little Morocco right here in the Florida swamp. (The Tequesta Indian name for the place is Opatishawock-alocka, which means "big swamp." Curtiss wisely shortened the name to Opa-Locka.)

Curtiss hired German architect Bernhardt Muller to design the city. A hotel, zoo, train station, and airport were completed before the land boom went bust and work stopped.

Today new buildings have to comply with the Moorish theme. There aren't many new buildings, however; downtown Opa-Locka is plagued by crime and drugs. But in its day, the city was a place even a sultan would admire.

Opa-Locka:

Urban blight has not erased this south Florida city's unique—and totally unexpected—Moroccan charm.

you know you're in
florida when...
...you're contemplating your navel

You can't think of Florida without thinking of oranges. (Or, at least, the Florida Citrus Commission hopes you can't.)

A big, orange orange is featured prominently on Florida license plates. Motorists are encouraged to stop for a cup or two of orange juice at welcome centers on the state's border. There is even a county in Florida named after the ubiquitous fruit.

Florida's connection to oranges is understandable. Citrus is a $9 billion industry in the state, employing 90,000 people. In a typical (non-hurricane-battered) year, Florida citrus trees produce 22 *billion* pounds of fruit, making Florida by far the nation's leading producer of citrus.

The orange, of course, is the undisputed king of Florida citrus. Florida grows 70 percent of America's oranges, 90 percent of which are squeezed into juice at huge processing plants like the Tropicana plant in Bradenton. The most popular squeezing orange is the Valencia, but there are at least six other varieties grown commercially in the state, including the sweet-sounding (and tasting) Pineapple Orange, the Parson Brown, and the Honeybell.

Say what you want about Christopher Columbus; he did at least one thing right. The much-maligned explorer brought the first orange seeds and seedlings to the New World from Spain around the year 1500. By

Oranges:

The undisputed kings of Florida citrus are such a big part of the state's economy that they're even featured on our license plates.

the 1820s, when Florida became a U.S. territory, there were orange groves thriving as far north as St. Augustine. (Subsequent freezes moved the orange's growing zone much farther south.)

Although the orange is a great source of vitamin C—indeed, it is the primary source for most Americans—the sweet fruit has taken a hit lately from the low-carb crowd. Let us remind dieters that a 12-ounce glass of orange juice contains 110 percent of the daily recommended allowance of vitamin C, plus vitamins A, B1, and B6, calcium, folic acid, iron, magnesium, and potassium. Even better, eating just one medium-size orange provides 28 percent of your daily fiber.

Take that, Coca-Cola!

The Panhandle region of Florida, extending west nearly to Mobile, Alabama, is more "southern" than south Florida. There are more young natives and fewer northern retirees. More grits and fewer bagels. The drawls can be as thick as those grits, and the Civil War is still sometimes referred to as the "Wah of Nawthun Aggreshun."

The Florida capital is part of the Panhandle, but state representatives from Miami are far closer to Havana (90 miles) than they are to Tallahassee (480 miles).

(Traveling from one end of Florida to the other is quite a slog. It's a 792-mile drive from Pensacola to Key West. You'd make better time driving from Pensacola to Cincinnati, Ohio, which is only 719 miles away.)

If the southeastern United States made geographical sense, Florida's capital would be near Orlando and the Panhandle would be part of Alabama. What's often forgotten in state history is that this division almost happened after the "wah." Florida offered to sell the territory to Alabama. The war-depleted Cotton State couldn't come up with the money, so the Panhandle coastline, now known as the "Redneck Riviera," remained a part of Florida.

The confusion, and perhaps insecurity, is reflected in some Panhandle town names. In the northwestern-most section of Florida, you will find such places as Vicksburg, Union, Nixon, Two Egg, Cairo, and Ponce de Leon.

All this antebellum color helps explain why it's sometimes said in Florida that if you want to go south, go north.

The Panhandle:

This home of the "Redneck Riviera" almost became a part of Alabama.

PANHANDLE

you know you're in
florida when...
...you're going batty

In the days before aerial spraying of insecticides, people turned to more creative and natural ways to control Florida's abundant mosquito population.

At least that's one way to explain the Perky Bat House on Sugarloaf Key.

Richter Clyde Perky was one of the biggest landowners in the Florida Keys in the 1920s. He founded a town on Sugarloaf Key called, unimaginatively enough, Perky. The centerpiece of the town was a fancy fishing resort to which wealthy tourists from New York and other points north were transported aboard Henry Flagler's new overseas railroad to Key West.

Perky (the resort) would have been a perfect vacation destination but for one thing: It was plagued by swarms of vicious, bloodsucking mosquitoes. Perky (the man) decided to do something. Acting upon advice in a book titled *Bats, Mosquitoes, and Dollars,* Perky began construction of a giant bat roost in March 1929. The 30-foot-high, unpainted wooden tower was built behind what is now Sugarloaf Lodge at a cost of $10,000. The stubby, shingled pyramid with a louvered door to allow the mosquito-eating bats in and out sits on four legs and looks a little like a wooden rocket ship waiting to take off.

Perky Bat House:

A 1920s developer built a bat tower to control the island's mosquito population. Unfortunately, the bats never arrived.

The bats, apparently, were looking for something more, so Perky mixed up some bat bait. The redolent gruel consisted of bat poop mixed with the ground-up sex organs of female bats. Suffice it to say you would not have confused the aroma with orange blossoms.

Bats, to their credit, never came near the place.

Today the Perky Bat House still stands, batless as ever, behind Sugarloaf Lodge at mile marker 17. Who knows? Maybe Perky should have tried Key lime pie.

you know you're in
florida when...
...you're suddenly overcome by tacky urges

They're pink, they're plastic, they're tacky . . . and we want some!

How did pink flamingo lawn ornaments become so popular, and what accounts for our sudden lapse in taste?

Blame the phenomenon on Don Featherstone. (And tourists. You can pretty much blame anything on tourists.) In the 1920s, when everyone was flocking to Florida to invest their money in worthless swampland, the pretty pink flamingo became the symbol of our muggy little piece of paradise. Photos were taken and circulated, and by the 1950s the Pepto-Bismol-colored bird was an icon of middle-class America.

The first flamingo lawn ornament, created in the 1940s by the Union Plastics Company of Massachusetts, was a two-dimensional thing that never really took flight. Enter Featherstone, a 21-year-old sculptor and classical art student, who made a clay sculpture of a flamingo based on photographs in *National Geographic*. The rest, as they say, is kitsch history.

The first neon-pink molded plastic lawn flamingos went on sale in 1957 and were an immediate sensation. Americans bought millions of them. Then came the 60s, when all those buyers opened their eyes and said, "Whoa! What were we thinking?"

Pink Flamingos:

These kitschy lawn icons of the 1950s are now considered—dare we say it?—art.

Pink flamingo lawn ornaments languished in obscurity until the mid-1980s, when a combination of nostalgia and the TV show *Miami Vice* made the things popular again.

Featherstone never got any royalties for his amazing creation, but he did become vice president of Union Plastics, and in 1987 the company started embossing its flamingos with his signature. "I'm getting my name pressed into the rump of every bird that goes out the door," Featherstone proudly told an interviewer.

We think we're going to cry . . .

you know you're in
florida when...
...you're reading *The Yearling*

Marjorie Kinnan Rawlings was a college-educated journalist who fled New York to live in the middle of nowhere in north-central Florida.

It turned out to be a good move. Drawing inspiration from the beautiful, unspoiled countryside and the simple, uneducated Florida "crackers" who lived there, Rawlings wrote *Cross Creek, The Sojourner,* and her masterpiece, *The Yearling,* which won a Pulitzer Prize in 1939.

Rawlings named her 72-acre homestead Cross Creek because it was situated between Orange Lake and Lochloosa Lake. During the 13 years she spent there, Rawlings went entirely native. She cooked three meals a day on a wood-burning stove and washed her clothes in an iron pot. She grew her own herbs and vegetables and tended flocks of chickens, a pair of mules, and a cantankerous dairy cow named Dora, whose rich, creamy milk belied her foul personality.

The locals were wary of Rawlings at first but eventually grew to trust her and invite her into their lives. Rawlings filled notebook after notebook with what she saw and heard, distilling her notes into elegant, poignant, and often humorous books about a hardscrabble people who could seldom read her words.

The Marjorie Kinnan Rawlings State Historical Site, located near Hawthorne, is the place to go to learn more about this remarkable woman, who corresponded with Robert Frost and F. Scott Fitzgerald when she wasn't milking her cow or stirring a tasty pot of greens. As you tour the original house and outbuildings, you get the sense that time is still something for other people to worry about. For more information call (352) 466–3672.

Marjorie Kinnan Rawlings:

This New York journalist went native in backwoods Florida and wrote several spellbinding novels about a Florida that is no more.

Some people might be offended to be called a redneck, but not the good folks of Chumuckla, a small town (wide spot in the road is more like it) in the Panhandle.

In fact, town residents love rednecks so much that they throw an annual parade in their honor. Called, appropriately enough, the Chumuckla Redneck Parade, it got its start when some good ol' boys got into the Jack Daniel's on Christmas Eve some time ago and had to be led home by their wives. Some parade, somewhere, has probably been inspired by less, but we can't think of one offhand.

"It started as a joke," said parade coordinator Kathy Barr, "but it caught on and kept growing."

Today nearly 10,000 people from as far away as Dothan, Alabama, and Fort Walton Beach come to watch or participate in the Redneck Parade. It's held every year on the second Sunday in December.

Even city slickers are welcome to participate in the Redneck Parade. All you need to do is make a $1.00 donation and contribute a food item for the needy. Before you sign up, though, it would be a good idea to go out and buy yourself a sturdy set of Bubba Teeth. For the benefit of the orthodontically unimpaired, Bubba Teeth are splayed, discolored fake choppers with more gaps than the Nixon tapes. Think of the dental work of the hillbillies in *Deliverance,* and you've got a pretty good picture. Bubba Teeth, needless to say, are available in all of the finer convenience stores and minimarkets in and around greater Chumuckla.

Feel free to create your own redneck-themed float. (If your idea is Santa Claus in a bathtub pulled by a go-kart, be advised it's already been done.)

Chumuckla is located about 25 miles northeast of Pensacola on County Road 182. Don't blink, or you'll miss it; there's not even so much as a traffic light. For more information on the Redneck Parade, call Kathy Barr at (850) 994–5505.

Rednecks:

In the Panhandle town of Chumuckla, rednecks are the guests of honor at an annual parade.

you know you're in
florida when...
...sand sculpting is an art

Once upon a time in Florida, you overturned a plastic bucket of wet sand upon the beach, decorated the resultant mound with a seashell or two, and called it a sand castle.

The investment of energy was minimal, no one's back got overly sunburned, and there was plenty of time left for a trip to the 'gator-wrestling show.

Well, in case you haven't noticed, times have changed. Today sand castle–building is a competitive sport. Yes, sport. There is even a governing organization (the World Sand Sculpture Association) that oversees professional tournaments in which prize money—yes, prize money—is awarded.

We would be indignant and highly disapproving of this trend were it not for the fact that a professionally made sand castle is a work of art. Yes, art. The masters of the craft have gone way beyond grainy turrets and spires into the realm of portraiture, landscapes and, in at least one instance, the Great Wall of China (not as long as the real thing, but quite impressive nonetheless).

Though constructions may be more sophisticated than before, the two main ingredients of a successful sand castle remain the same: water and sand. Here's one of the secrets to building a really cool sand cre-

Sand Castles:

Building castles out of sand has become more than a pleasant beach diversion. There are now professional sand sculptors, and they compete for real money.

ation: Make a big mound of wet sand and construct your castle (or octopus or airplane or Mona Lisa) from the top down. Building from the ground up results in shaky walls and is a doomed effort. Use whatever tools you need, up to and including a dental pick, to complete your project. (Keep in mind that the works of pros and amateurs alike eventually fall prey to high tide.)

The American Sandsculpting Festival is held the first weekend in November on Fort Myers Beach. Pros and amateurs may participate. Call (941) 454–7500 for more details.

you know you're in
florida when...
...you feel something sharp between your toes

If only the weed were as popular as its name.

There is a Sandspur restaurant and a Sandspur Motel. Sandspurs is the name of a band and a Tampa volleyball club. The Rollins College newspaper in Winter Park is called the *Sandspur*.

Branding is all well and good, but when people walk barefoot into a patch of sandspurs, their initial thoughts are unlikely to have anything to do with grouper sandwiches or feisty editorials.

"Ouch!" is the usual response, or something considerably stronger if a sandspur happened to find the sensitive webbing between the toes, which it invariably does.

Sandspurs are common across the southern tier of states, from North Carolina to California, but the place that seems to make them happiest is a white, powdery Florida beach. The combination of sun, dry sand, and abundant tender flesh produces giant, malevolent sandspurs that could have starred in *Little Shop of Horrors*.

To call sandspurs "weeds" does not really do them justice. Gardeners, farmers, picnickers, and beach strollers call them "Nature's little land mines" or something more colorful. The seed head of the sandspur is what does the dirty work. There are between 6 and 20 sharp, spiky burrs in a

seed head, each one just waiting to attach itself to your skin, shoes, clothing, or pet. (Nothing rounds out a day at the beach better than plucking 500 deeply embedded sandspurs from the coat of your golden retriever.)

Pensacola Beach has such a vigorous and abundant crop of sandspurs that a local bar began sponsoring an annual Sandspur Contest. The person who finds the biggest, most malicious sandspur wins a free pizza.

If the more colorful aspects of sandspurs are lost on you, you can fight back by pulling them up by hand (not fun) or replacing infected areas with fresh sod (also not fun). Or do what we do, and drown 'em in Roundup. It feels surprisingly good.

Sandspurs:

The name may be catchy, but you definitely don't want to find one of these thorny burrs in your flip-flops.

...something tastes fishy

Florida is known for its great seafood. Grouper, crab, shrimp, scallops, oysters ... you name it, Florida's got it. Probably the best way to sample a wide variety of seafood is to visit one or more of the state's many seafood festivals. Here's a list of some of the more popular ones.

Cortez Commercial Fisherman's Festival (Cortez, February). Mullet is the main food. Call (941) 794–1249.

Fort Myers Beach Shrimp Festival and Parade (Fort Myers Beach, March). Shrimp is the main food. Call (239) 463–9738 or (239) 463–6986.

Palm Beach Seafood Festival (West Palm Beach, March). Food includes shrimp, oysters, crawfish, grouper, crab, and more. Call (561) 832–6397.

Seafest (Cape Canaveral, March). Food includes fish and shellfish. Call (321) 459–2200.

Marathon Seafood Festival (Marathon, March). Food includes dolphin, shrimp, lobster, crab, oysters, and clams. Call (305) 743–5417.

RajunCajun Seafood Festival (Ovieda, April). Crawfish is the main food. Call (407) 384–9211.

Seafood Festivals:

Seafood festivals are a great way to sample Florida's abundant treats from the deep. There's not a festival every weekend; it just seems that way.

SEAFOOD FESTIVAL
FLORIDA

Pompano Beach Seafood Festival (Pompano Beach, April). A variety of fresh seafood is featured. Call (954) 570–7785.

Cotee River Seafood Festival (New Port Richey, May). A variety of fresh seafood is featured. Call (727) 842–8066.

Florida Seafood Festival (Apalachicola, November). Food includes oysters and crab. Call (888) 653–8011.

you know you're in
florida when...
...you suffer from the Sanibel Stoop

On the islands west of Fort Myers, you sometimes see otherwise healthy-looking people walking bent at the waist, as if suffering from some painful arthritic condition.

Don't feel too sorry for these folks. Their hunchback shape is merely the result of a temporary condition called the Sanibel Stoop, a stiffening of the back resulting from long hours of combing the white sands of Sanibel Island in search of seashells.

Sanibel and the island just to its north, Captiva, offer some of the best shelling in Florida. Part of the reason is the way the island is situated, and another part is the absence of offshore sandbars, which means incoming waves can roll in unfettered and deposit their colorful cargo of olives, tulips, and whelks upon the beach.

But this is, after all, Florida, so probably the biggest reason Sanibel Island is considered the state's ultimate shelling destination is that some clever man or woman at the local chamber of commerce put out the word to the media that it is so.

Don't get us wrong. Sanibel and Captiva Islands offer great shelling; there are some nice restaurants in the area; and it's a great place to vacation if hurricanes aren't threatening, which they tended to do a lot in the fall of 2004. We're just saying that you can collect nice shells on beaches all over

Seashells:

The islands west of Fort Myers offer some of the best shelling in the state. Bring sunscreen and limber up your back.

Florida, and if you want to say you found them on Sanibel, chances are nobody will doubt your word.

Important warning! The seashells you see layering the beach were once (and possibly still are) the homes of soft-bodied animals called mollusks. Not only is it illegal to collect seashells with live critters inside, but after a bucket of the things bake in the hot trunk of your car for a day or so, you will wish you had chosen to vacation in the mountains instead.

That said, about all you need to gather seashells is a bucket, a hat, a pair of sunglasses, about a gallon of sunblock, and a strong back. Just try not to collide with any of your fellow Sanibel Stoopers.

Walking along the Gulf beaches near Venice should serve as a reminder to brush and floss every day.

Hundreds of thousands of fossilized shark teeth, ranging in size from ⅛ inch to more than 3 inches, lie buried in the pepper-colored sand. (The black particles are ground-up fossils.) The teeth are all that remain of sharks that lived in this part of the world millions of years ago. (Much of Florida was under water back then, which means that shark teeth and other fossils often can be found far inland.)

Though shark teeth vary in color from black to brown to gray, depending on the minerals in the soil in which they were buried, the thing they have in common is abundance. Sharks of all species continually shed their teeth and grow new ones. In 10 years, an average tiger shark can produce 24,000 teeth.

How you hunt for shark teeth depends on your level of commitment. You can get down on your hands and knees and paw through the sand with your hands; you can sift the sand with a colander; you can scout along the edge of the surf for freshly uncovered teeth; or you can don snorkel or scuba gear and really make a project of it.

The city of Venice calls itself the Shark Tooth Capital of the World. Every August the Venice Area Chamber of Commerce stages its Shark Tooth and Seafood Festival near the municipal airport. If you're in town, stop by the Chamber at 597 South Tamiami Trail; the staff will give your kids a free little bag of shark teeth.

Whether you follow this up with flossing and brushing instructions is up to you.

Shark Teeth:

The fossilized chompers of sharks that lived millions of years ago are there for the picking on Venice beaches. It's the safest way to get close to a shark's tooth.

It is not true that the theme music from the 1975 movie *Jaws* fills the air every time a swimmer steps into the Florida surf.

But it is, unfortunately, true that more shark attacks occur in Florida's coastal waters than any other place on Earth. Thirty shark attacks were recorded in Florida in 2003, accounting for approximately one-third of the world's total. (Attack-wise, 2004 was an off year due to multiple hurricanes scaring away beachgoers.)

Florida doesn't necessarily have more sharks circling off its coast—it's just that there are more human targets paddling around in the warm surf. Most shark attacks occur on the state's east coast; an inlet near New Smyrna Beach that is popular with surfers is a particularly dangerous place.

The threat of a shark attack, however, should not alter your vacation plans. You're much more likely to die from drowning, a lightning strike, or a bee sting than you are from a shark attack. (This was meant to sound reassuring, but somehow it didn't come off that way.)

You can lessen your chance of being bitten by staying out of the water at dusk and during the night, not wearing flashy jewelry while swimming, and not swimming in areas where people are fishing or spear-fishing.

Sharks:

Florida has more shark attacks than anyplace else, but you're more likely to die from a bee sting.

Despite their fearsome reputation, sharks may prove to be of benefit to humans. Scientists at the Center for Shark Research at Mote Marine Laboratory in Sarasota are studying sharks' remarkable wound-healing abilities, their natural resistance to cancer, and the fact that they are relatively disease-free.

Although this might be difficult if one is clamped onto your leg, you should actually feel sorry for sharks. More than 100 million are killed each year. In some cases, only the dorsal fin is taken for shark fin soup, an Asian delicacy.

That's no way to treat a movie icon.

you know you're in
florida when...
...you're pushing a disc

If you wanted to come up with a symbol for retirement living in Florida, the shuffleboard court could be it.

Shuffleboard is still popular with the senior set, but not nearly as much as it used to be. Back in the 1930s and 40s, St. Petersburg was the shuffleboard hub of the universe. The St. Petersburg Shuffleboard Club, the oldest and at one time the largest in Florida, boasted 4,000 members in its heyday following World War II. There were dozens of courts, a grandstand area with lights for evening play, and stadium seating for 400 spectators.

Today the club is more of a historical footnote than a community gathering place. Membership is down to fewer than 200 people, the courts are empty most of the time, and the facility is starting to show its age. (It didn't help when the World Shuffleboard Hall of Fame moved from St. Petersburg to Clearwater.)

Originally called Shovelboard or Shoveboard, shuffleboard began as a board game similar to what's found in bars and arcades today. It was popular in England as early as the 15th century, especially among the aristocracy. It is said that King Henry VIII banned his archers from playing the game because it was cutting into their archery practice.

Much later, shuffleboard became a popular deck game on cruise ships. The land-based variation was introduced around 1913 at Daytona Beach. Shuffleboard quickly gained in popularity and spread rapidly through the United States, particularly in retirement communities.

Even Hollywood was not immune to the charms of shuffleboard. Such stars as Betty Grable, Harry James, Merv Griffin, and Alan Ladd were known to shove a disc every now and then.

As new residents flock to Florida, maybe they will discover the joys of shuffleboard and help the sport reclaim its popularity. At least if it cuts into archery practice today, nobody's likely to complain.

Shuffleboard:

The game that is synonymous with retirement was a favorite among some Hollywood celebrities.

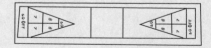

you know you're in
florida when...
...there is a town for bearded ladies

Half a century ago, people who made their living as sideshow "freaks" wintered in a small town on the bay just south of Tampa. While walking to the post office or grocery store in Gibsonton, it wasn't unusual to run into a bearded lady, a three-legged man, or a human "blockhead" famous for hammering ice picks up his nose.

Most of these people are old or dead now, but the Gibsonton circus tradition lives on. Many residents of this unpretentious town of 7,000 are ticket takers, clowns, acrobats, animal trainers, or ride mechanics.

Al Tomaini and his wife, Jeanie, helped establish Gibsonton in the 1940s. Al, better known as The Giant, was 8 feet, 5 inches tall. Jeanie, otherwise known as Half Girl, was 2 feet, 6 inches tall. The Giant and Half Girl are gone, but the restaurant they started, Giant's Camp, remains a fixture alongside the Tamiami Trail. (Be sure to try the biscuits; they're homemade.)

Inside the restaurant are pictures of some of Gibsonton's more famous winter residents, including Percilla the Monkey Girl, the Anatomical Wonder, and Lobster Boy. The Siamese twin Hilton sisters, who ran a fruit stand, are also pictured.

Sideshow performers came to Gibsonton not only because of the mild climate but also because of lenient zoning laws that

Sideshow Town:

Located just south of Tampa, Gibsonton is a traditional home of circus folk.

allowed them to keep elephants and circus trailers on their front lawns. The post office even has a counter designed especially for dwarfs.

Next to Giant's Camp is one of the Giant's enormous boots. Like the rest of the town, it's looking more than a little frayed.

Unless you're an NBA recruiter, 8-foot 5-inch humans apparently aren't that big of a deal anymore.

...you smell something that's definitely not orange blossoms

If you are wandering around the woods at night in eastern Sarasota County and encounter something large, hairy, and smelly that isn't your husband (or wife!), do not run screaming back to your trailer park.

Instead, calmly remove your camera from your pocket, check to make sure you have film, wait for the flash to power up, and then take a picture of the thing.

Because at this point, the photo record of the legendary Florida skunk ape is pretty dismal. It consists only of a few blurry shots—taken by an elderly Sarasota woman—that could be of a large carnivorous anthropoid or a shaggy bush; it's really hard to say.

The Florida skunk ape is a cousin of Bigfoot (aka Sasquatch) and possibly a distant relative of the Yeti, though opinion remains divided on that question. First reported in Lakeland in 1947, the skunk ape made irregular appearances thereafter in the Everglades, Myakka State Park, along the Manatee River, and in an area of southern Manatee County that is now Lakewood Ranch.

Experts say that the skunk ape is somewhat smaller than Bigfoot and considerably more aromatic. Think of an overgrown orangutan that is Right Guard challenged.

How can you arrange for a close encounter with a skunk ape? First, find a woodsy area that is reasonably close to a trailer park. (It's unclear why skunk apes are attracted to trailer parks. Perhaps, years ago, a resident invited one in to watch *Planet of the Apes*.) Next, string some apples between two trees. (Skunk apes go ape over apples.) Then just sit back and wait. If you hear "womp" noises and get a whiff of something that smells like it just died, then either you are in the presence of a skunk ape or your companion ate too many beans for dinner.

Either way, take a picture. Undiscovered large anthropoidal science needs all the evidence it can get.

Skunk Apes:

Supposedly they're big, they're hairy, and they smell bad. Football players badly in need of a shower? Think again.

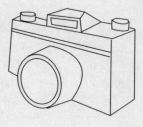

you know you're in
florida when...
...birds of a different feather arrive each winter

They migrate south at the first hint of cold weather and form large flocks at golf courses and early-bird specials.

It's easy to make fun of snowbirds, but the nearly one million seasonal residents who winter in Florida have a significant impact on the state's economy.

According to a study by the University of Florida (UF), the average snowbird is likely to be a New Yorker, older than 55, and healthier and wealthier than retirees who call Florida home year-round.

Forty-three percent of snowbirds have college degrees, and 35 percent have incomes of more than $100,000, compared to 35 percent of state residents who are college educated and 11 percent whose incomes are more than six figures.

Snowbirds stay in Florida for an average of five months, creating a multibillion-dollar economic boom that restaurateurs and retailers refer to as "The Season."

According to the UF study, New Yorkers account for 13.1 percent of Florida's seasonal residents, followed by people from Michigan (7.4 percent), Ohio (6.7 percent), and Pennsylvania (5.8 percent). Canadians account for 5.5 percent of the snowbirds.

Most snowbirds flock to the southern part of the state. Lee County, in southwest Florida where Fort Myers is located, has the most seasonal residents, followed by Palm Beach, Miami-Dade, Collier, Broward, Polk, Pinellas, Sarasota, Pasco, and Hillsborough Counties.

During the height of The Season, roughly one out of every 17 people in Florida is a snowbird. It's something to think about the next time you hear a joke about someone driving slow in the left lane with his turn signal on.

Snowbirds:

They flock south to Florida at the first hint of cold weather. Some never go north again. Can you blame them?

you know you're in
florida when...
... you're among the beautiful people

If you don't like what South Beach is now, just wait. It's sure to be something else soon.

South Beach can transform itself faster than David Copperfield. In the 1870s the southern portion of Miami Beach between 1st and 23rd Streets was a coconut grove. During the land boom of the 1920s, millionaires such as Harvey Firestone and J. C. Penney built a 3-mile stretch of mansions along Collins Avenue called "Millionaires Row." Then, in 1926, a major hurricane wiped out just about everything.

South Beach was reborn again during the Depression when another new group, mostly Jewish, built a number of small, art deco hotels along lower Collins Avenue and Ocean Drive.

In the 1970s and 80s, South Beach was primarily a retirement community. Most of its artsy oceanfront hotels and apartments were filled with elderly people living on fixed incomes.

It wasn't until the late 1980s that South Beach began taking on the look we know today. The fashion industry discovered this enchanting, luminous spit of sand, and soon it was the preferred backdrop for some of the world's most famous fashion photographers.

South Beach:

This playground for the rich and famous (and those who like to gawk at them) was once a coconut grove.

Today you can hardly take a step without encountering a top model or someone in her entourage. South Beach is the place to go if you want to see and be seen. As sports go, people-watching is to South Beach what soccer is to England.

The nightclub scene begins at 11:00 P.M. and goes to . . . whenever. Places with names like Honey, Opium, and B.E.D. contribute to South Beach's reputation as a world-class entertainment district.

Our mommies don't allow us to stay out that late, but South Beach also has some excellent restaurants that open long before Letterman comes on. Try to get a window seat; there's a great view.

you know you're in
florida when...
...you're rolling backward uphill

You don't have to travel to outer space to experience anti-gravity; the sensation is available next to an elementary school in Lake Wales.

The story of Spook Hill goes like this: Once upon a time, at a place not far from what is now a convenience store, an Indian town near Lake Wales was plagued by a huge alligator. The town's great warrior chief and the gator were killed in a titanic struggle that created the huge, swampy depression nearby. The chief was buried on the north side of the depression.

Later, pioneer haulers coming from the old Army trail atop the ridge found their horses laboring here, at the foot of the ridge, and called the place Spook Hill. (Legends are often maddeningly stingy with details.)

Is it the gator seeking revenge, or is the chief protecting his land?

Does any of this make sense to you?

Who cares, because the fun of Spook Hill is sitting in your car as it rolls . . . uphill. Or at least that's the way it seems. A sign near the bottom of the hill on North Wales Drive instructs you to stop on the white line and put your car in neutral. Your eyes tell you you're headed downhill, but your car tells you otherwise.

Spook Hill:

An Indian chief and an alligator may be responsible for a localized suspension of the laws of gravity.

Be sure to check your rearview mirror for cars behind you before you investigate the optical illusion that is Spook Hill; not only do you roll backward, but you do so briskly.

Spook Hill is located just down the hill from the intersection of North Wales Drive and Burns Avenue. Small brown signs scattered about town direct you to the place. Right around the corner is Spook Hill Elementary School, the logo for which is, appropriately enough, a ghost.

Mind your speed when driving by the school in the morning or afternoon. The tickets the cops hand out are no optical illusion.

you know you're in
florida when...
... you're watching a baseball game in winter

If you're a baseball fan, the month of March means one thing: spring training.

The 18 (as of this writing) major-league teams that play spring training games in Florida are known collectively as the Grapefruit League. (The league's counterpart in Arizona is called the Cactus League.)

Although the games are played primarily for practice and as a way to evaluate new talent, they are wildly popular with fans. More than 1.6 million tickets were sold in 2004, most of them for games played in stadiums holding fewer than 7,000 seats.

The Florida tradition began in 1914 when St. Petersburg's former mayor, Al Lang, convinced Branch Rickey to move his St. Louis Browns to the Sunshine State for spring training. Al Lang Field, which was recently renamed (over our objections) Progress Energy Park, is still a great place to watch a ball game. You can sit in the sun or the shade, and there's a great view of sparkling-blue Tampa Bay beyond the left-field wall. Given enough beer and sunshine, you might even see the ghosts of Babe Ruth, Lou Gehrig, and Mickey Mantle—just a few of the baseball legends who played at Al Lang.

Unfortunately, the small-town charm of spring training is quickly becoming a thing of the past. Big, expensive stadiums are replacing the rickety wooden structures of yore, and ticket prices are soaring. The Boston Red Sox, who won the 2004 World Series and play their spring-training games at City of Palms Park in Fort Myers, upped 2005 spring-training ticket prices to $44 for premium seats.

But when it's 20 degrees in Boston and you're sitting shirtless in the Florida sun, watching a ball game, things like that seem to matter less.

Spring Training:

The Boys of Summer come to Florida in March to get in shape for the regular season.

The stone crab habitat stretches from North Carolina to Belize, but most people have never heard of the creatures, much less eaten them, until they come to Florida.

The first time you swish a giant, meaty claw through a puddle of melted butter, you'll agree it was worth the trip. The flavor of stone crab is somewhere between that of lobster and blue crab. All the meat is in the claws, which look like Popeye's forearms and, when attached to the living creature, are strong enough to crush clam shells.

What makes stone crabs unusual is that they aren't killed when they're caught. After the crabs are hauled into the boat (in box-shaped traps), fishermen carefully snap off both claws and return each armless crab to the sea. In two or three years the crab will regenerate both its claws, which, with luck (ours, not the crab's), will again end up on a dinner plate.

People who are turned off by all the mess and fuss involved with eating blue crabs will have a much easier time with stone crabs. At restaurants, the claws are usually pre-cracked in the kitchen, so all you have to do is pick out the meat with a small fork and dip it directly into melted butter or mus-tard sauce. You can also buy stone crabs precooked at seafood markets.

Stone Crabs:

Florida lobsters don't have claws. With stone crabs, you eat the claws only. What a delicious paradox.

At home you can briefly heat cooked crabs in boiling water or serve them chilled, as most people prefer. Crack the claws with a stout mallet or hammer, taking care to wrap the claw in a clean dish towel first so shell shrapnel doesn't go flying across your kitchen. Melt some butter or mix equal parts of Dijon mustard with mayonnaise, and you're ready for a feast fit for a king.

Bon appétit!

OK, it's not really a strawberry; it's just a painting of one, atop the water tower in Plant City. But if there were an official World's Largest Strawberry, you'd probably find it here, in the self-described Winter Strawberry Capital of the World.

Plant City, in eastern Hillsborough County, is to strawberries what Indian River is to oranges and Apalachicola is to oysters. More than 20 percent of America's straw-berries are grown in or around Plant City and the neighboring counties of Pasco, Polk, and Manatee. In February, when much of the rest of the nation is battling snow-drifts, growers in Plant City are picking and shipping strawberries with evocative names like Oso Grande, Sweet Charlice, and Rosa Linda.

In early March Plant City hosts an annual Strawberry Festival that dates back to 1930. The festival features a strawberry shortcake–eating contest, a strawberry-picking contest, and, of course, the crown-ing of Miss Strawberry.

Plant City is not, as you might expect, named after the ubiquitous strawberry plant. It's named after Henry Plant, a bigshot railroad tycoon who fixed the little town up with its first set of tracks back in 1885.

Quick strawberry trivia question: How do you know that you have no life? Answer: When your idea of a good time is counting the number of seeds on a strawberry. We'll save you the trouble: The average number is 200.

Strawberries:

While people in the Northeast are shov-eling snow, Floridians are digging into bowls of fresh-picked strawberries. There is, needless to say, a festival cele-brating that fact.

you know you're in
florida when...
...you're getting a sugar buzz

It calls itself "America's Sweetest Town," which you have to admit sounds better than "America's Town Where It Gets So Hot in the Summer You Can Hardly Breathe."

Clewiston, a dot on the map just southwest of Lake Okeechobee, is the heart of Sugar Country. Most of America's sugar is grown in the rich, mucky soil surrounding the big lake. (The land was created when the Army Corps of Engineers installed dikes on the lake and dug channels to carry away excess water. It's a sore point with environmentalists to this day.)

The sugar industry took off in the late 1920s. Stewart Mott (of Mott's apple juice fame) was designing cars for General Motors when he learned that a struggling sugar company near Clewiston was up for sale. He bought the company, which later became U.S. Sugar Corp., the largest sugar company in America.

In case you've never seen sugarcane, it looks like a 15-foot-high, thick-stalked blade of grass. Sugarcane fields in the Clewison area are set afire in October to burn off the foliage. Then giant harvesters cut the cane and the stalks are sent to a mill where they are crushed, drained (they contain a lot of water), and refined into sugar or molasses.

The harvesting goes on 24 hours a day, seven days a week, for seven months.

Sugar:

A small town near Lake Okeechobee is the heart of the nation's sugar industry.

Christmas is the only day the great machines are silent.

There is, of course, a Sugar Cane Festival in Clewiston every year in late April. Exhibits show the way sugar was made in the days before giant factories and machines. There's also a dessert-making contest featuring—can you guess?—sugar. But the high point is unquestionably the crowning of Miss Sugar. If she is unable to perform her duties during the course of the year, she is presumably replaced by Miss Sweet'N Low.

To our knowledge, this has never happened.

you know you're in
florida when...
...you're watching the sun go down

Key West was once a haven for pirates. Over time it began attracting drifters, gypsies, hippies, real-estate speculators, and tourists.

The jury is still out on whether any of this is an improvement.

In any event, the one thing that everyone has in common is an appreciation of Key West's gorgeous sunsets. A colonoscopy is reason enough for a party in the southernmost area of the United States, so you can imagine how people act when the setting sun sizzles into the sea.

The festivities occur every evening (sun permitting) at Mallory Square, at the foot of Duval Street, arguably the partying-est boulevard in Florida. Legend has it that the famous playwright Tennessee Williams, gin-and-tonic firmly in hand, initiated the tradition by applauding the setting sun. (Presumably he put down his drink to do so.) By the 1960s the tradition had a name: Sunset Celebration.

Gin-and-tonics gave way to other things, to the point that some sunset appreciators swore they saw Atlantis rising out of the clouds at the end of day. Today the scene is bizarre enough without such aids. The setting sun competes for the crowd's attention with street vendors, jugglers, sword swallowers, contortionists, magicians, musicians, acrobats, and maybe even the ghost of Atlantis if atmospheric conditions are just right.

Keep your eye out for the flash of green light that allegedly occurs at the instant the sun slips below the horizon. If you miss it, the 1962 John D. MacDonald mystery *A Flash of Green* (or the 1984 movie version, filmed partially on Casey Key) is an excellent substitute.

The Mallory Square festivities begin about two hours before sunset. Just follow the crowd.

Sunsets:

Watching the sun slip below the horizon is a Florida pastime. Why do you think we moved here?

you know you're in
florida when...
...you're smearing on sunscreen

Florida is not called the Sunshine State for nothing.

The city of St. Petersburg, located in the middle of what is fittingly called the Suncoast, is nicknamed Sunshine City. It averages 361 sunny days a year, more than Honolulu. St. Petersburg is in the *Guinness Book of World Records* for having the longest consecutive run of sunny days— 768 from February 9, 1967, to March 17, 1969.

The St. Petersburg *Evening Independent* newspaper, printed for seventy-six years, was given away free on those rare days when the sun did not shine. When the Independent went out of business on November 8, 1986, it had been given away only 295 times, an average of less than four times a year.

Like so many other things, sunshine is a mixed blessing. It helps plants grow, including our lawns (which we have to mow incessantly during the summer), and it helps our bodies produce vitamin D, a vital nutrient. Unfortunately, too much sun can cause painful sunburn and skin cancers, including the potentially fatal malignant melanoma.

If you are working or playing outdoors in Florida's strong—and abundant—sunshine, dermatologists recommend that you use sunscreen with a sun protection factor (SPF) of at least 15.

A wide-brimmed hat and a good pair of sunglasses are not a bad idea, either. Flip-flops are optional.

Sunshine:

Florida has so much sunshine that a St. Petersburg newspaper used to give away free copies on every cloudy day. The paper went out of business, but not for that reason.

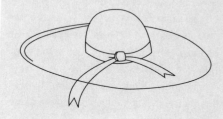

you know you're in
florida when...
...the Golden Gate Bridge seems short

The graceful lines of the Sunshine Skyway Bridge suggest a sheer yellow sail floating above the waters of Tampa Bay.

At 12,828 feet, the Skyway is the world's longest cable-stayed concrete bridge. (The Golden Gate Bridge, by comparison, is a mere 8,981 feet long.) Although drivers passing over it are sure to marvel at the Skyway's beauty, they may be unaware of the grim history predating its opening in April 1987.

The original Skyway, which opened in 1954, was the first bridge to connect St. Petersburg to Bradenton. It was joined by a twin span in 1971. Tragedy struck on May 9, 1980. During a violent early-morning rain squall, the giant phosphate freighter *Summit Venture* veered out of the shipping channel and struck the southbound span. A 1,261-foot section of bridge crumbled into the bay, killing 35 people, most of them passengers on a Miami-bound Greyhound bus that plummeted into the abyss. Of those who went over the edge, only one survived—the driver of a pickup truck that bounced off the deck of the freighter below.

What was left of the southbound span and the northbound span were eventually demolished. Portions of the bridges now serve as fishing piers.

Sunshine Skyway Bridge:

This graceful span across Tampa Bay was the scene of a tragic accident in 1980.

The new Skyway, which rises 193 feet over Tampa Bay, is built to withstand freighter impacts and also does away with the slippery, see-through steel grate at the top that used to make our hands grip the steering wheel a little tighter.

The beautiful new bridge is, in a way, a monument to those who died on that awful day in 1980.

you know you're in
florida when...
...you're hangin' ten

Hurricanes and tropical storms may terrify Florida homeowners and tourists, but there is one group that can't get enough of the big storms: surfers.

Although there are a few spots on the state's east coast that sport decent-size waves (Sebastian and New Smyrna Inlets being two of the most popular), it's the days just before the arrival of a hurricane that get Florida surfers thoroughly stoked. (After a hurricane it's often difficult for surfers—or anyone else—to make it to the beach due to road damage and debris.)

Swells that are typically a modest 2 or 3 feet high suddenly rear up to 10 feet or higher. Aside from surfers, the only people you see outdoors when a Category 3 hurricane is barreling ashore are TV weather reporters. The general public is divided as to which group is crazier.

But surfers can't really count on hurricanes to provide their wave-riding thrills (except in 2004, when there were plenty of storms to choose from). The next best thing is a winter nor'easter to kick things up, as winter waves are generally bigger than summer waves.

Surfing in Florida is usually low-key, but sometimes tempers flare. Surfers, particularly those working the inlets, often have to compete with fishermen who don't appreciate getting their lines cut or tangled

Surfing:

The waves tend to be gentle until a hurricane blows ashore. Then it's everyone into the water, 'cause surf's up!

by a board-rider when they've got a big bluefish on.

Florida is also the shark-attack capital of the world, and the areas on the east coast frequented by surfers are some of the most dangerous.

That being said, surfing is a very popular activity in Florida for beginners and pros alike. The year's big surfing tournament is the National Kidney Foundation Florida Surfing Festival and Contest, held every Labor Day weekend at Cocoa Beach. For more information on the festival, call (321) 449–0855 or visit www.kidneyfla.org/e_surf.html.

The Suwannee is a scenic 250-mile river that meanders south from Okeefenokee Swamp in Georgia to the Gulf of Mexico, forming (more or less) the eastern boundary of the Florida Panhandle.

However pretty it may be, the Suwannee was just another river until it was made famous by the 1851 hit single "Swanee River," also known as "Old Folks at Home."

The river's big break almost never happened. Composer Stephen Foster originally chose South Carolina's Pee Dee River as the song's namesake. Foster wisely decided that the lyric "Way down upon the Pee Dee River" might not capture the public's imagination; after consulting an atlas, he settled on the far more mellifluous Suwannee.

The atlas was as close as Foster ever came to the Suwannee, or to Florida, for that matter. Born in Pittsburgh in 1826, Foster spent his entire life in the North, where he became the most successful and prolific songwriter of his day. Besides "Old Folks at Home," he penned "Beautiful Dreamer," "Camptown Races," "Jeanie with the Light Brown Hair," and "My Old Kentucky Home," to name just a few.

Foster is to be credited—or blamed, depending on your point of view—with launching Florida's tourist industry.

"Swanee River" sold hundreds of thousands of copies, and starting in the late 1800s, folks from Up North began coming to Florida, seeking the quaint, happy plantation world that Foster made up for the purposes of his song. The tune had such an impact that the Florida legislature made it the official state song in 1935.

Unfortunately, Foster's use of dialect and choice of words reflected some of the prejudice of his day. The lyrics were updated in 1978 for the dedication of the new Florida capitol building.

Suwannee River:

Stephen Foster wrote a song about the river without ever laying eyes on it. Or Florida either, for that matter.

you know you're in
florida when...
...you're eating a tree

Swamp cabbage doesn't sound all that delectable, which could explain why epicures prefer to call the stuff "hearts of palm."

Either way, swamp cabbage is nothing more than the bud—or heart—of the cabbage palm, the official state tree of Florida. (This is a rather curious designation since the cabbage palm is not a tree at all, but more closely related to grass.) In the good old days, Florida crackers subsisted on swamp cabbage, usually including it in a meal of fried mullet and hush puppies. (Cholesterol was not an issue back then.)

To obtain swamp cabbage you must, unfortunately, kill the cabbage palm. Cut through the trunk about 12 inches below the lowest row of fronds. Then slowly (and laboriously) trim away the tough, fibrous outer husk of the trunk until you reach the white, tender "bud" of the tree.

What you do next is pretty much up to you. You can cut the heart of the palm into thin strips and serve it in a salad. Or, you can do as the crackers did and boil some chunks in a couple of cups of water and then mix it with bacon grease and fried bacon.

The cabbage palm is abundant throughout Florida, but if you want to hack one down in the wild to obtain swamp cabbage, you must first obtain official authorization from the state. (Presumably, if you buy one from a nursery, you can have your way with it.)

It pretty much goes without saying that Florida has a Swamp Cabbage Festival. It's held in LaBelle the last weekend of February on the banks of the Caloosahatchee River. Besides offering a variety of swamp cabbage dishes, there's a parade, a rodeo, and plenty of bluegrass music. But the unquestioned highlight of the event is the crowning of Miss Swamp Cabbage.

Miss America, eat your heart out. So to speak.

Swamp Cabbage:

It seems like a lot of work for a vegetable with little or no taste, but for Florida pioneers it was a staple of life.

you know you're in
florida when...
...the word *Tamiami* makes sense

Some call it a blight; others call it a connection with Florida's past. However you feel about it, if you visit southwest Florida, you will almost certainly drive on the Tamiami Trail.

Opened in 1928, the 275-mile highway got its name because it connects Tampa with Miami. (We thought it was stupid at first, too, but it kind of grows on you.) Along the way, the road passes through such cities and towns as Ruskin, Bradenton, Sarasota, Punta Gorda, and Naples. Much (too much) of that section is the typical urban American landscape of banks, gas stations, convenience stores, and chain restaurants.

The Trail, as it's known to locals, gets more interesting when it turns to the east at Naples. Very soon the view changes from flashing signs and parking lots to tall, swaying grass, soaring hawks, and fat alligators basking in the sun. You are now entering the Everglades.

The 'Glades part of the Trail can be spooky to drive at night. The road is narrow, and many eyes reflect back at you from the swamp. It is not a good place to have a breakdown. But if you drive it during the day, it can be fun. There's plenty of wildlife to see and lots of airboat rides to choose from. You know you're nearing the end of the swamp when you see the 10-story Miccosukee Resort and Gaming Center shimmering in the distance.

Tamiami Trail:

This old highway was the first to connect Tampa with Miami. The drive through the Everglades is as spooky as ever.

The Tamiami Trail was an engineering marvel in its time. It took 12 years to build and cost a whopping $8 million. The hardest portion to build, by far, was the 75-mile section through the Everglades. The bugs, bogs, alligators, and snakes made for dangerous work. Many tons of dynamite were used to break up the limestone subsurface, which was then hauled off by ox-pulled carts to help form the roadbed.

The Tamiami Trail begins near Ybor City in Tampa and ends just beyond Miami's Eighth Street, *Calle Ocho,* in the heart of Little Havana. The highway is so cool that Bill Haley and His Comets even did a song about it in 1960 called, appropriately enough, "Tamiami."

Nobody's likely to do that for Interstate 75.

you know you're in
florida when...
...you're sponging

Tarpon Springs is now the place you go for great Greek food and pastries, including sinfully rich baklava.

But the place wasn't always all about moussaka and spanakopita. In the late 1800s Tarpon Springs was an exclusive winter resort for wealthy northerners. (The woman who named the place mistook leaping mullet for the much larger game fish. Whether ouzo was involved in this confusion is anyone's guess.)

In 1887 one of the small town's promoters discovered that money could be made by harvesting and selling the abundant live sponges living in the nearby Gulf of Mexico. The industry grew quickly, and it wasn't long before Tarpon Springs was known as the Sponge Capital of the World. In fact, for 30 years the sponge industry was the largest industry in Florida—bigger than citrus or even tourism.

Sponges are collected by hand by divers in bulky suits who receive their air supply from pumps aboard a boat floating above. By the early 1900s Greek fishermen, whose sponging heritage goes back centuries, had moved to Tarpon Springs and essentially taken over the industry. By 1905 more than 500 Greek spongers were working on a fleet of 50 boats.

The industry thrived north of Tampa Bay until the 1940s, when the sponge beds

Tarpon Springs:

Once the Sponge Capital of the World, this lively Greek community is now better known for its markets and fine restaurants.

were destroyed by bacteria and artificial sponges entered the market. It wasn't until the 1980s, when healthy beds were discovered farther out in the Gulf, that Tarpon Springs once again became the leader in natural sponge harvesting.

Today the sponge docks are busy with tourists who stop by the many Greek restaurants, bakeries, and sponge shops. If you go, be sure to visit Spongeorama (510 Dodecanese Boulevard; 727–938–5366). It's a delightfully retro tourist attraction that teaches you all that you could possibly want to know about sponging. Best of all, it's free.

94

It took less than 20 years for central Florida's Marion County to be transformed from swampland into America's second-leading breeder of thoroughbred race-horses.

In 1943 Carl Rose, the owner of a highway construction business, realized that the area's limestone bedrock, which he used to build roads, might also help build strong-legged racehorses. (Similar rock formations are found beneath the ground in Lexington, Kentucky, the nation's leading producer of thoroughbreds. Calcium in the rock fortifies the soil and water and is believed to harden the horses' bones.)

Rose built Ocala's first horse farm, Rose-mere Farm, and other farms soon followed. In 1957 a thoroughbred named Needles became the first Florida-bred horse to win the Kentucky Derby. (Spindly as a colt, Needles got his name because of his frequent visits to the vet.)

Today 10,000 people work on 60,000 acres of horse farms in and around Ocala. Sleek horses working out or grazing in emerald-green, white-fenced pastures are easily seen from Interstate 75, which cuts through Marion County.

Strong legs are important because the 1,600-pound animals gallop on legs that are barely thicker than a man's. Drinking the mineral-laden water helps, but exercise is also important. When they're not running around tracks, the horses get toned further by swimming in giant, heated indoor pools.

Many Ocala-bred thoroughbreds wind up running at one of Florida's racetracks, such as Calder Race Course in Miami or Tampa Bay Downs in Oldsmar. (Hialeah Park, unfortunately, is out of business.)

For more information on this subject, read Charlene R. Johnson's excellent book *Florida Thoroughbred.*

Thoroughbred Horses:

The green, rolling pastures around Ocala are home to some of the nation's finest racing horses.

you know you're in
florida when...
...you have visions of gold

"Once you've seen the ocean bottom covered with gold coins, you'll never forget it!"

We'll have to take Mel Fisher's word on that, but he certainly should know. Fisher grew up in Indiana and got the itch for treasure hunting by reading *Treasure Island*. One of the pioneers in scuba diving, Fisher eventually moved to Key West to search for the sunken Spanish treasure ship *Atocha*. That vessel and its sister ship, the *Santa Margarita*, sank in a 1622 hurricane about 40 miles southwest of Key West.

Fisher and his crew, the Treasure Salvors, had previously combed the ocean floor between Melbourne and Fort Pierce for remains of the famed "Plate Fleet," a convoy of 11 Spanish galleons that had sunk in the hurricane of 1715. Some silver coins from those wrecks occasionally wash up on area beaches, but the bulk of the treasure has never been found.

Fisher had better luck with the *Atocha*. On July 20, 1983, after years of searching, one of his dive teams came across what looked like a reef made of rocks. It turned out to be a towering stack of more than 1,000 silver bars.

The treasures that Fisher and the Salvors recovered from the *Atocha* and *Santa Margarita* wrecks are estimated to be worth

Treasure Hunting:

The reefs along Florida's east coast and the Keys are where many treasure-laden Spanish galleons found a watery grave. In 1983 Mel Fisher found the Big One.

$200 to $400 million. The haul included 127,000 silver coins, 900 silver bars averaging 70 pounds apiece, 250 pounds of gold bars, 700 emeralds, and hundreds of artifacts, many of which have found their way into private collections.

Fisher died in 1998, but some of his more eye-popping finds remain available for public viewing at the Mel Fisher Maritime Museum (200 Greene Street, Key West; 305–294–2633).

you know you're in
florida when...
...you're kissing a fish

The pink kissing gourami that's making eyes at you from the other side of the aquarium glass was probably raised in a Florida pond.

Likewise the red velvet swordtail, the black mollie, and the silver angel.

Florida is the leading producer of tropical fish in the United States. There are more than 200 fish farms in the state, most of them south and east of Tampa. Hundreds of varieties of tropical fish and ornamental aquatic plants are grown in approximately 20,000 small, shallow ponds, each pond containing anywhere from 50 to 1,000 fish.

It can be a dicey business. Farmers have to constantly monitor water quality and test for diseases. A severe winter cold snap can devastate the industry, and birds like egrets, herons, and kingfishers are always lurking in hope of an easy lunch.

The Florida tropical fish industry dates back to the 1930s, when fish were shipped north via railroad in steel milk containers. Air shipment revolutionized the industry in the 1960s, and today tropical fish are the second largest air-freight item at Tampa, Miami, and Orlando International Airports. More than a million boxes of live tropical fish are shipped out of Florida annually.

Different kinds of fish are raised in different parts of the state based on soil and water conditions. In south Florida, for example, the hard coral-rock subsurface means that breeders must build their fish ponds aboveground.

The biggest demand for Florida tropical fish is in the winter, when folks in the northeast are indoors more and in need of some form of entertainment other than *Beverly Hillbillies* reruns.

A pink kissing gourami can be awfully seductive when it's snowing outside.

Tropical Fish:

Florida leads the nation in the breeding of tropical fish. Perhaps our kissing gouramis just don't know when to say no?

you know you're in
florida when...
...fish walk on land

When they first appeared in Florida in the 1960s, they were dubbed "Frankenfish."

And why not? Anyone who has seen a walking catfish wriggle out of a muddy ditch and undulate across a road can be excused for thinking he or she has come face-to-fin with a fish of extraterrestrial origins.

Walking catfish are native to Southeast Asia and probably made their way to Florida as part of the tropical fish trade. They proliferated quickly in the many lakes, ponds, and low wet spots that characterize Florida, and within 10 years they had spread to 20 counties in the south and central parts of the state.

Walking catfish "walk" with the help of their stiff pectoral fins. Spongy lung-like organs allow them to breathe air and to thrive in stagnant ponds where other fish can't.

Walking catfish are probably the most bizarre of the 34 (as of this writing) exotic fish species that have found new homes in Florida. Four consecutive hurricanes that hit the state in 2004 created the kind of wet conditions that allow these 14-inch critters to move from lake to lake and bog to bog.

The fish are especially active on rainy summer nights. Driving on the Tamiami Trail through the Everglades, you might encounter entire schools of the critters crossing the road. This has not happened to us, but others say that if you hit the fish, it's like driving on an oil slick.

We realize that is not a good segue, but walking catfish are very good to eat. Prepare them as you would any other catfish (dredge in corn meal, deep fry, repeat as needed), and try not to think of the fact that you are eating fish that came from some other, very weird part of the galaxy.

Walking Catfish:

No, you're not seeing things. This non-native species can wiggle and squirm across the street into another pond. They're not bad eating, either.

you know you're in
florida when...
...you're watching a mermaid show

It's not easy being a mermaid. You go through one year of on-the-job training, and the final exam consists of holding your breath underwater for two and a half minutes while changing out of your costume in the mouth of a fast-gushing, 72-degree spring.

Oh, and did we mention the tail?

Weeki Wachee is the brainchild of Newton Perry, a former U.S. Navy frogman who in 1946 came up with the idea of having pretty women in mermaid suits stay underwater and breathe through an air hose fed by an air compressor. (Hey, somebody invented pet rocks, too. Inspiration can be a mysterious thing.)

The shows, which began in 1947, are still popular today. Nineteen mermaids dance underwater (a ballet based on Hans Christian Andersen's "The Little Mermaid" is one of the standard pieces) and demonstrate how to eat and swig RC Cola while holding their breath. Since the mermaids perform in a real spring, the shows sometimes feature unrehearsed appearances by actual wildlife, including manatees and alligators. Visitors watch it all unfold from the safety of a glass-walled auditorium built 16 feet below the surface of the spring.

At the park, which is located near Spring Hill, you can also take a riverboat ride, float

Weeki Wachee:

At this theater the performers dance underwater and eat and drink there, too. But it's becoming a mermaid that's the really tough part.

on a tube down the Weeki Wachee River, or ride the flume at Buccaneer Bay Water Park.

If all of this sounds kind of corny to you, be advised that Elvis once took in the mermaid show at Weeki Wachee. So there.

Weeki Wachee Springs is located at the intersection of U.S. Highway 19 and State Road 50. For more information, call (352) 596–2062 or visit http://mermaid.weeki wachee.com.

you know you're in
florida when...
...you're in the presence of one big, honkin' gator

Since Florida is home to a million alligators, it's only fitting that the World's Largest Gator lives here, too.

"Lives" might be a bit of an exaggeration given that the World's Largest Gator has never moved, grunted, or eaten a marshmallow. But it is unquestionably big. At 200 feet, 1 inch long, the artificial gator covers the gift shop, ticket counter, and offices at Jungle Adventures, an old-timey tourist attraction near the small town of Christmas.

Sadly (or not sadly, depending on your point of view), the Christmas gator out-measures what once reigned as the World's Largest Gator, the 126-foot inanimate beast adjacent to Alligatorland Safari Zoo in Kissimmee. The Kissimmee gator does get valuable style points for having a fake safari Jeep in its jaws, from which dangles on a rope an equally fake explorer. Kitschy Florida does not get any better than this.

If size still matters to you after all of this, consider taking a trip to the St. Augustine Alligator Farm Zoological Park to see Gomek, or at least the stuffed version of him. Gomek is (was) a 17½-foot, 2,000-pound Indopacific crocodile. Until he died in 1997, Gomek was the undisputed star of the Farm, one of the oldest tourist attractions in the state. He was fed mullet and whole chickens. For a between-meals snack, he would occasionally eat some of

World's Largest Gator:

Where else but Florida would you expect to find this beast? Wisconsin? No, that would be the World's Largest Muskie.

the smaller gators in his aquarium that were too slow or too stupid to get out of his way. It was—from Gomek's perspective, at least—a good life.

Today Gomek's enormous stuffed carcass is ensconced in its own shrine-like hut on the grounds of the Farm. The croc's huge mouth is agape, and he looks ready to run down any chicken—or tourist—that ventures too near.

you know you're in
florida when...
...the smell of money is in the air

When Bubba wants a six-pack, he goes to the 7-Eleven store on the corner. When Lily Pulitzer wants a new watch, she goes to Worth Avenue and buys a Cartier Pasha for $15,000.

Who says the rich are different from you and me? (Well, actually, F. Scott Fitzgerald said it, but what did he know?)

Worth Avenue is where Palm Beach millionaires (and people who want people to think they're millionaires) go to shop. Don't look for a Sears or JCPenney here (although J. C. Penney, the man, did build a mansion along Palm Beach's Millionaires Row). Among the 200 shops you'll find such names as Gucci, Giorgio Armani, Louis Vuitton, and, of course, Cartier. Many people actually buy the expensive clothing, jewelry, and fine leather goods sold here, but others—tourists, mostly—just like to breathe in the ambience, which, not surprisingly, smells a lot like money.

In 1918 Addison Mizner, a talented architect who had traveled the world, built the swank Everglades Club at the foot of Worth Avenue, which at the time was still a dirt road. The Everglades Club staged weekly luncheon fashion shows in which the latest clothes from around the world were paraded on enormous runways. Elizabeth Arden, Sarah Fredericks, and Bonwit Teller were among those who took turns outfitting the shows.

After the shows were over, the ladies would take to the stores to shop.

Little has changed to this day, except the prices. Some of the stores in Worth Avenue show off their wares by appointment only. If you're staying at The Breakers, Palm Beach's landmark hotel, ask the concierge for assistance.

Because it would be so *déclassé* to dial the phone yourself. Heck, you might break a nail.

Worth Avenue:

This posh Palm Beach shopping district draws the rich and famous and those who like to gawk at them.

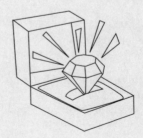

index